GARDEN of GRAPES.

Second Edition: 2024

Published by Garden of Grapes.

Printed in USA

Library of Congress Cataloging-in-Publication Data:

Second Edition.

Disclosure: for the Second Edition of Our Cookbook
In this second edition of our cookbook, we have carefully curated the recipe list, removing less-than-stellar options and rearranging the photographs to create a more visually appealing layout. Additionally, we have included 10 bonus recipes that we believe you will enjoy. Throughout this process, our goal has been to provide you with an even more exceptional culinary experience.

Manufactured in USA

Introduction

Welcome, culinary enthusiasts and adventurers, to "The Saudi Arabian Home Cook: Taste Saudi Arabia's Rich Heritage - A Middle Eastern Cookbook with 100+ Recipes and Stunning Pictures." Within these pages, you'll uncover the essence of Saudi Arabian cuisine, a tapestry woven from the rich cultural heritage and vibrant flavors of this majestic land.

This cookbook serves as a gateway to the heart of Saudi Arabian cooking, inviting you to savor the authentic flavors and experience the warmth of traditional Saudi Arabian hospitality. Each recipe is a testament to the country's diverse culinary landscape, offering a glimpse into the time-honored techniques and cherished ingredients that have shaped Saudi Arabian cuisine for generations.

My inspiration for creating this cookbook stems from a deep appreciation for the culinary traditions of Saudi Arabia and a desire to share its rich tapestry of flavors with the world. Having had the privilege of experiencing the warmth and generosity of Saudi Arabian home cooks, I wanted to create a collection of recipes that would capture the essence of their kitchens and allow readers to embark on their own culinary adventures.

So, dear readers, prepare to tantalize your taste buds and embark on a culinary journey through the flavors of Saudi Arabia with "The Saudi Arabian Home Cook." Whether you're a seasoned chef or a curious novice, this cookbook promises to inspire your creativity, broaden your culinary horizons, and transport you to the heart of the Middle East. Bon appétit, and may your kitchen be filled with the rich aromas and vibrant flavors of Saudi Arabian cuisine!

Cooking Philosophy or Approach

In the vibrant tapestry of Middle Eastern cuisine, where spices mingle and aromas dance, "The Saudi Arabian Home Cook" emerges as a culinary oasis, inviting you to embark on a gastronomic journey through the rich and diverse flavors of Saudi Arabia. With over 100 recipes that capture the essence of this ancient land, this cookbook serves as a tribute to the rich heritage and culinary traditions that define Saudi Arabian cuisine.

Our approach to cooking and food is steeped in a deep reverence for the culinary traditions of Saudi Arabia, rooted in the rich tapestry of history and culture that has shaped the nation's cuisine. We celebrate the abundance of flavors and ingredients that grace Saudi Arabian tables, from the bold spices of the Arabian Peninsula to the fragrant herbs and succulent meats that are staples of the Saudi diet. Each recipe is a celebration of the culinary artistry that defines Saudi Arabian cuisine, offering a glimpse into the rich tapestry of flavors that have been passed down through generations.

But what truly sets "The Saudi Arabian Home Cook" apart is its emphasis on home cooking and the intimate connection between food and family. Each recipe is a labor of love, inspired by the cherished traditions and memories that have been handed down through generations. From hearty stews and aromatic rice dishes to indulgent desserts and refreshing beverages, every dish tells a story of tradition, hospitality, and the joy of sharing a meal with loved ones.

So gather your ingredients, fire up your stove, and let "The Saudi Arabian Home Cook" be your companion on a culinary journey through the flavors of Saudi Arabia. Here's to savoring the rich heritage and vibrant flavors of this ancient land, one delicious recipe at a time.

Tips for Successful Cooking

Welcome to The Saudi Arabian Home Cook, a culinary journey that invites you to savor the rich and diverse flavors of Saudi Arabian cuisine. Within the pages of this Middle Eastern cookbook, you'll embark on an exploration of over 100 authentic recipes that celebrate the vibrant culinary heritage of Saudi Arabia. Accompanied by stunning pictures that capture the essence of Saudi culture and cuisine, this cookbook is your guide to experiencing the warmth, hospitality, and flavors of Saudi Arabian cooking in your own kitchen.

But before we dive into the delectable recipes that await, let's take a moment to appreciate the culinary heritage of Saudi Arabia—a land where ancient traditions, cultural influences, and modern innovations converge to create a cuisine that is as diverse as it is delicious.

First and foremost, let's talk about the heart of Saudi Arabian cuisine: spices and seasonings. From the warm embrace of cinnamon and cloves to the bold flavors of cumin and coriander, spices play a central role in Saudi cooking, infusing each dish with layers of flavor, depth, and complexity. In The Saudi Arabian Home Cook, you'll learn how to use these aromatic treasures to create dishes that are as bold and flavorful as they are comforting and satisfying.

Next, let's explore the bounty of the land and sea. Saudi Arabia's diverse landscape—from the fertile valleys of the Hijaz region to the Red Sea coast—provides a wealth of fresh ingredients that form the foundation of its culinary repertoire. From succulent lamb and aromatic rice to fresh seafood and vibrant produce sourced from local markets, every ingredient reflects the natural abundance and gastronomic diversity of Saudi Arabia.

tradition and family. In Saudi culture, food
symbol of hospitality, generosity, and
meal with family and friends or hosting a
Home Cook offers a treasure trove of
ople together, foster bonds, and create
able.

splendor of Saudi Arabian cuisine. In The
photographs accompany each recipe,
the palate. From colorful mezze platters
nd refreshing beverages, each image is a
of Saudi food culture.

adventure with The Saudi Arabian Home
oustling markets, vibrant souks, and warm
meal is a celebration of flavor, tradition,
re's to tasting Saudi Arabia's rich heritage
eriences that will linger in your heart long

Kitchen Essentials

In the bustling kitchen of Saudi Arabian culinary tradition, mastering the art of cooking begins with the right tools at your disposal. Here are five essential kitchen companions that will accompany you on your flavorful journey through the kingdom's rich heritage, along with expert tips on how to wield them effectively:

Essential Kitchen Tools:

1. Chef's Knife:
A stalwart companion in any culinary endeavor, the chef's knife is your versatile ally in the kitchen. From precise dicing to confident slicing, invest in a high-quality chef's knife with a sharp blade to effortlessly tackle a variety of ingredients, from delicate herbs to hearty vegetables.

2. Mortar and Pestle:
Embrace the age-old tradition of spice blending with a mortar and pestle, a timeless duo that unlocks the full potential of aromatic ingredients. Grind whole spices to release their essential oils and elevate your dishes with layers of flavor that pay homage to Saudi Arabia's culinary heritage.

3. Heavy-Duty Griddle:
Whether you're searing meats to perfection or toasting flatbreads with a golden crust, a heavy-duty griddle is an indispensable tool in the Saudi Arabian kitchen. Opt for a durable cast iron or stainless steel griddle that distributes heat evenly, ensuring consistent results every time.

4. Tagine:
Transport yourself to the sun-drenched landscapes of the Arabian Peninsula with a traditional tagine, a clay pot with a conical lid that gently simmers ingredients to tender perfection. Ideal for slow-cooked stews and aromatic braises, the tagine infuses your dishes with layers of flavor and aromatic complexity.

Kitchen Essentials

Tips for Effective Use:

1. Knife Skills:
Master the art of knife work by practicing proper technique, including the pinch grip for optimal control and the rocking motion for swift and precise cuts. Keep your chef's knife sharp with regular honing and sharpening to effortlessly glide through ingredients without crushing or tearing.

2. Mortar and Pestle Mastery:
Harness the power of your mortar and pestle by choosing the right size for the task at hand—opt for a larger mortar for grinding spices in batches and a smaller one for crushing garlic and herbs. Use a gentle, circular motion to grind spices to the desired consistency, adjusting the pressure as needed to release their full flavor potential.

3. Griddle Guidance:
Achieve perfect sears and caramelization on your griddle by preheating it thoroughly before adding ingredients. Control the heat to prevent burning and ensure even cooking, flipping your meats and vegetables at the halfway point for uniform doneness.

4. Tagine Techniques:
Embrace the slow-cooking magic of the tagine by layering ingredients strategically to promote even heat distribution and maximize flavor infusion. Keep the lid on during cooking to trap steam and moisture, adjusting the temperature as needed to maintain a gentle simmer.

Armed with these essential tools and expert tips, you're ready to embark on a culinary adventure that honors the rich heritage of Saudi Arabian cuisine. Happy cooking!

Flavor Pairing Suggestions

Welcome to "The Saudi Arabian Home Cook," a culinary treasure trove where we invite you to taste the rich and diverse heritage of Saudi Arabia through over 100 authentic recipes accompanied by stunning pictures. In this Middle Eastern cookbook, we embark on a flavorful journey that celebrates the unique flavors, traditions, and hospitality of Saudi Arabian cuisine.

Before we delve into the mouthwatering recipes that await, let's take a moment to appreciate the cultural richness and culinary traditions that inspire each dish. Saudi Arabian cuisine is a reflection of the country's history, geography, and diverse cultural influences, blending flavors from the Arabian Peninsula, Persia, and beyond. From aromatic spices and succulent meats to fragrant rice dishes and irresistible desserts, each recipe offers a glimpse into the vibrant tapestry of flavors that define Saudi Arabian cooking.

So, dear reader, prepare to embark on a culinary odyssey that will tantalize your taste buds and transport you to the heart of Saudi Arabia. With "The Saudi Arabian Home Cook" as your guide, let's explore the delicious flavors and rich heritage of Saudi Arabian cuisine, one mouthwatering recipe at a time.

Table of content

Chapter 1: Mezze Marvels

6 servings   15 minutes

Easy

Hummus with Olive Oil Drizzle

Ingredients:

2 cans chickpeas,
1/2 cup tahini,
2 cloves garlic,
lemon juice,
salt,
olive oil,
paprika

Creamy Delight
Hummus, a Middle Eastern staple, is a creamy delight made from chickpeas, tahini, and aromatic spices. This versatile dip has ancient origins, dating back to Egyptian and Levantine cuisines, where it was enjoyed for its rich flavors and nutritional benefits.
Savor the creamy goodness of Hummus with Olive Oil Drizzle and experience the timeless appeal of this beloved dip.

Directions

1. Drain and rinse chickpeas.
2. Blend chickpeas, tahini, garlic, lemon juice, and salt until smooth.
3. Adjust seasoning to taste.
4. Transfer to a serving bowl and drizzle with olive oil and sprinkle paprika before serving.

Insider Tips

Tahini - Almond butter, Chickpeas - Cannellini beans

Baba Ganoush with Pomegranate Seeds

Normal

Ingredients:

2 large eggplants,
1/4 cup tahini,
2 cloves garlic,
lemon juice,
salt,
pomegranate seeds,
parsley

Smoky Elegance
Baba Ganoush, a smoky eggplant dip, is a culinary delight with origins in the Levant region. Roasted eggplant, tahini, and garlic blend together to create a velvety dip that's both elegant and flavorful. Topped with vibrant pomegranate seeds, Baba Ganoush adds a touch of color and sweetness to any mezze spread.
Indulge in the smoky elegance of Baba Ganoush with Pomegranate Seeds and elevate your appetizer game.

Directions

1. Roast eggplants until tender and charred.
2. Scoop out flesh and blend with tahini, garlic, lemon juice, and salt.
3. Adjust seasoning to taste.
4. Transfer to a serving bowl and top with pomegranate seeds and parsley before serving.

Insider Tips

Tahini - Cashew butter, Eggplants - Zucchini

Easy

Labneh and Za'atar Dip

Ingredients:

2 cups labneh,
2 tablespoons za'atar,
olive oil,
salt,
pepper

Tangy Perfection
Labneh, a tangy yogurt cheese, pairs beautifully with za'atar, a Middle Eastern spice blend. This simple yet flavorful dip is a favorite in Mediterranean cuisine, offering a refreshing and zesty accompaniment to breads and vegetables.
Experience the tangy perfection of Labneh and Za'atar Dip and add a burst of flavor to your mezze platter.

Directions

1. Mix labneh with za'atar, olive oil, salt, and pepper.
2. Adjust seasoning to taste.
3. Transfer to a serving bowl and drizzle with olive oil before serving.

Insider Tips

Labneh - Greek yogurt, Za'atar - Dried thyme

8 servings   **60 minutes**

Stuffed Grape Leaves (Warak Enab)

Ingredients:

1 jar grape leaves,
1 cup rice,
1 onion, parsley,
mint,
lemon
juice,
olive oil,
salt,
pepper

Normal

Savory Delight
Stuffed Grape Leaves, also known as Warak Enab,
are a savory delight filled with rice, herbs, and spices.
This traditional Middle Eastern dish is a symbol of
hospitality and is often enjoyed as part of mezze
platters or main courses.
Delight your taste buds with the savory flavors of
Stuffed Grape Leaves and explore the culinary
heritage of the Levant.

Directions

1. Rinse grape leaves and blanch in boiling water.
2. Cook rice with onions, parsley, mint, lemon juice, olive oil, salt, and pepper.
3. Place a spoonful of rice mixture on each grape leaf and roll tightly.
4. Arrange stuffed grape leaves in a pot, add water, and cook until tender.
5. Serve hot or cold.

Insider Tips

Grape leaves - Cabbage leaves, Rice - Quinoa

Muhammara (Red Pepper and Walnut Dip)

Easy

Ingredients:

2 roasted red peppers,
1 cup walnuts,
2 tablespoons pomegranate molasses,
1 tablespoon olive oil,
garlic,
cumin,
red pepper flakes,
salt

Nutty Spice
Muhammara, a red pepper and walnut dip, is a nutty delight with origins in Syrian and Lebanese cuisines. Roasted red peppers, walnuts, and spices come together to create a flavorful dip that's both rich and spicy. Perfect for spreading on bread or dipping vegetables.
Indulge in the nutty spice of Muhammara and add a burst of flavor to your mezze platter.

Directions

1. Blend roasted red peppers, walnuts, garlic, pomegranate molasses, olive oil, and spices until smooth.
2. Adjust seasoning to taste.
3. Transfer to a serving bowl and drizzle with olive oil before serving.

Insider Tips

Pomegranate molasses - Balsamic glaze,
Walnuts - Almonds

Falafel with Tahini Sauce

~~~~~~~~~~~~~~~~~~~

4 servings   60 minutes

Normal

Ingredients:

1 cup dried chickpeas, soaked and drained
1 onion, chopped
3 cloves garlic
1/4 cup fresh parsley
1 tsp ground cumin
1 tsp ground coriander
Salt and pepper to taste
Oil for frying

Falafel, a beloved Middle Eastern dish, features crispy chickpea patties served with creamy tahini sauce, offering a perfect balance of flavors and textures.

Directions

1. Blend chickpeas, onion, garlic, parsley, cumin, coriander, salt, and pepper until smooth.
2. Form into patties and fry until golden.
3. Serve with tahini sauce and enjoy!

Insider Tips

Canned chickpeas can be used instead of dried.
Fresh cilantro can be used instead of parsley.
Use ready-made tahini sauce for convenience.

Easy

Fattoush Salad

Ingredients:

2 cups mixed greens
1 cucumber, diced
1 tomato, diced
1/2 red onion, thinly sliced
1/4 cup chopped parsley
1/4 cup chopped mint
1/4 cup olive oil
2 tbsp lemon juice
1 tsp sumac

Fattoush Salad, a refreshing Lebanese dish, combines crisp vegetables, toasted pita, and a tangy sumac dressing, creating a vibrant and flavorful salad.

Directions

1. Combine greens, cucumber, tomato, onion, parsley, and mint in a bowl.
2. Whisk together olive oil, lemon juice, and sumac.
3. Toss salad with dressing and top with toasted pita.
4. Serve immediately.

Insider Tips

Replace sumac with paprika for a similar tangy flavor.
Use any available greens for variety.
Add feta cheese for extra richness.

4 servings　　**30 minutes**

Kibbeh Nayyeh (Raw Minced Meat with Bulghur)

Easy

Ingredients:

250g lamb or beef, finely minced
1/2 cup fine bulghur
1/2 onion, finely chopped
1/4 cup chopped fresh mint
1/4 cup chopped fresh parsley
Salt and pepper to taste

Kibbeh Nayyeh, a traditional Lebanese dish, features raw minced meat mixed with bulghur and spices, served as an appetizer or part of a mezze spread.

Directions

1. Mix minced meat, bulghur, onion, mint, parsley, salt, and pepper until well combined.
2. Form into patties or balls.
3. Serve with pita bread and enjoy!

Insider Tips

Use ground meat if minced meat is not available.
Add a pinch of cumin for extra flavor.
Serve with yogurt sauce for a creamy twist.

6 servings

40 minutes

Moutabal (Eggplant and Tahini Dip)

Ingredients:

2 medium eggplants
1/4 cup tahini
2 cloves garlic, minced
2 tbsp lemon juice
2 tbsp olive oil
Salt and pepper to taste
Chopped parsley for garnish

Normal

Moutabal, a creamy eggplant dip, is a staple in Middle Eastern cuisine, combining smoky roasted eggplant with tahini and lemon juice for a flavorful dip.

Directions

1. Roast eggplants until soft and charred.
2. Scoop out flesh and mix with tahini, garlic, lemon juice, olive oil, salt, and pepper.
3. Garnish with parsley and serve with pita.

Insider Tips

Use store-bought roasted eggplant for convenience.
Add a pinch of cayenne pepper for a spicy kick.
Garnish with pomegranate seeds for a festive touch.

8 servings · **45 minutes**

Spinach Fatayer (Savory Pastry)

Ingredients:

500g spinach, chopped
1 onion, finely chopped
1/4 cup pine nuts
2 tbsp olive oil
1 tsp sumac
Salt and pepper to taste
Pizza dough or pastry dough

Normal

Spinach Fatayer, a popular Lebanese pastry, features a savory filling of spinach, onions, and pine nuts, wrapped in soft dough and baked to golden perfection.

Directions

1. Sauté onions in olive oil until translucent.
2. Add spinach, pine nuts, sumac, salt, and pepper, and cook until spinach is wilted.
3. Roll out dough and fill with spinach mixture.
4. Bake until golden brown.

Insider Tips

Use frozen spinach if fresh is not available.
Replace pine nuts with chopped almonds or walnuts.
Add feta cheese for extra richness.

Chapter 2: Soups and Stews

4 servings   40 minutes

Easy

Lentil Soup with Lemon

Ingredients:

1 cup dried lentils
4 cups vegetable broth
1 onion, chopped
2 carrots, diced
2 celery stalks, chopped
3 garlic cloves, minced
1 lemon, juiced
2 tbsp olive oil
Salt and pepper to taste
Fresh parsley for garnish

Lentil Soup with Lemon is a comforting dish that traces its origins to the heartwarming kitchens of Middle Eastern homes. This soup combines earthy lentils with zesty lemon, creating a harmony of flavors that soothes the soul. Whether enjoyed as a starter or a hearty meal, this soup is a testament to the timeless appeal of simple yet delicious ingredients. Get ready to savor the warmth and goodness in every spoonful of this delightful soup.

Directions

1. In a pot, heat olive oil and sauté onions, carrots, celery, and garlic until tender.
2. Add lentils and vegetable broth. Bring to a boil, then simmer for 30 minutes.
3. Season with salt, pepper, and lemon juice.
4. Garnish with fresh parsley before serving.

Insider Tips

Replace vegetable broth with chicken broth for a non-vegetarian version.
Use lime juice if lemon is unavailable.

Shorbat Adas (Middle Eastern Lentil Soup)

4 servings   45 minutes

Normal

Ingredients:

1 cup brown lentils
4 cups vegetable broth
1 onion, chopped
2 carrots, diced
2 celery stalks, chopped
3 garlic cloves, minced
1 tsp cumin
1 tsp coriander
1 lemon, juiced
2 tbsp olive oil
Salt and pepper to taste
Fresh cilantro for garnish

Shorbat Adas, or Middle Eastern Lentil Soup, is a culinary treasure cherished for its simplicity and robust flavors. Originating from the ancient kitchens of the Middle East, this soup features hearty lentils cooked to perfection with aromatic spices. With each spoonful, you'll experience the warmth of cumin, coriander, and a hint of tanginess from lemon. Prepare to be transported to the sun-kissed lands of the Middle East with this soul-nourishing soup.

Directions

1. Heat olive oil in a pot and sauté onions, carrots, celery, and garlic until softened.
2. Add lentils, vegetable broth, cumin, and coriander. Simmer for 30-35 minutes.
3. Season with salt, pepper, and lemon juice.
4. Garnish with fresh cilantro before serving.

Insider Tips

Use red lentils if brown lentils are unavailable.
Substitute cilantro with parsley if desired.

4 servings **60 minutes**

Harira (Moroccan Chickpea Soup)

Ingredients:

1 cup cooked chickpeas
1 can diced tomatoes
4 cups vegetable broth
1 onion, chopped
2 carrots, diced
2 celery stalks, chopped
3 garlic cloves, minced
1/4 cup chopped fresh parsley
1/4 cup chopped fresh cilantro
1 tsp cumin
1/2 tsp cinnamon
Pinch of saffron
2 tbsp olive oil
Salt and pepper to taste
Lemon wedges for serving

Normal

Harira, a beloved Moroccan Chickpea Soup, is a celebration of flavors inspired by the vibrant markets of Morocco. This hearty soup is a medley of chickpeas, tomatoes, and fragrant spices like cumin and cinnamon. Traditionally enjoyed during Ramadan, Harira nourishes both body and soul, making it a cherished dish in Moroccan cuisine. Get ready to embark on a culinary journey with each spoonful of this soul-warming soup.

Directions

1. In a pot, heat olive oil and sauté onions, carrots, celery, and garlic until soft.
2. Add chickpeas, tomatoes, vegetable broth, cumin, cinnamon, and saffron. Simmer for 45 minutes.
3. Stir in parsley, cilantro, salt, and pepper.
4. Serve hot with lemon wedges.

Insider Tips

Use canned chickpeas for convenience. Turmeric can be added for extra color and flavor.

4 servings   50 minutes

Easy

Chicken and Rice Soup

~~~~~~~~~~~~~~~~~~

Ingredients:

2 boneless, skinless chicken breasts
4 cups chicken broth
1 onion, chopped
2 carrots, diced
2 celery stalks, chopped
1/2 cup white rice
3 garlic cloves, minced
1 tsp dried thyme
1 bay leaf
Salt and pepper to taste
Fresh parsley for garnish

Chicken and Rice Soup is a classic comfort dish that has warmed hearts for generations. Originating from homely kitchens around the world, this soup combines tender chicken, hearty vegetables, and fluffy rice in a savory broth. Whether enjoyed on a chilly evening or as a soothing remedy for colds, this soup is a timeless favorite that brings warmth and nourishment to the table. Prepare to indulge in a bowl of cozy goodness with every spoonful of this delightful soup.

Directions

1. In a pot, combine chicken broth, chicken breasts, onion, carrots, celery, garlic, thyme, and bay leaf. Bring to a boil, then simmer for 20-25 minutes until chicken is cooked.
2. Remove chicken, shred it, and return to the pot.
3. Add rice and simmer until tender.
4. Season with salt and pepper.
5. Garnish with fresh parsley before serving.

Insider Tips

Use rotisserie chicken for a shortcut.
Substitute brown rice for white rice if preferred.

4 servings   **45 minutes**

Normal

Okra and Lamb Stew

mmmmmmm

Ingredients:

1 lb lamb,
1 onion,
2 cloves garlic,
1 cup chopped tomatoes,
1 cup okra,
2 cups beef broth,
1 teaspoon cumin,
1 teaspoon paprika,
salt,
pepper,
olive oil

Hearty Comfort

Okra and Lamb Stew is a hearty comfort dish with roots in Middle Eastern and Mediterranean cuisines. This stew combines tender lamb, flavorful spices, and succulent okra for a wholesome meal that warms the soul.

Indulge in the comforting flavors of Okra and Lamb Stew and experience the timeless appeal of home-cooked goodness.

Directions

1. Heat olive oil in a pot and brown lamb pieces.
2. Add chopped onions and garlic, sauté until fragrant.
3. Stir in chopped tomatoes, cumin, paprika, salt, and pepper.
4. Add beef broth, cover, and simmer for 30 minutes.
5. Add okra to the stew and cook until tender.
6. Adjust seasoning if needed and serve hot.

Insider Tips

Okra - Green beans, Lamb - Beef

1 serving **50 minutes**

Normal

Freekeh Pilaf with Chicken

~~~~~~~~~~~~~~~~~~~

Ingredients:

1/2 cup freekeh,
1 chicken breast (cut into pieces),
1 onion (chopped),
2 cloves garlic (minced),
1 cup chicken broth,
Salt and pepper to taste,
Olive oil

Freekeh Pilaf with Chicken is a hearty Middle Eastern dish featuring tender chicken and nutty freekeh grains.

Directions

1. Heat olive oil in a pan. Saute onions and garlic until golden. Add chicken pieces and cook until browned.
2. Add freekeh and chicken broth. Season with salt and pepper.
3. Cover and simmer until freekeh is cooked and chicken is tender.

Insider Tips

Use quinoa instead of freekeh for a gluten-free option.

1 serving   **40 minutes**

Samak Harra (Spicy Fish Stew)

Easy

Ingredients:

1 fish fillet (such as tilapia or cod),
1 onion (chopped),
2 tomatoes (chopped),
2 garlic cloves (minced),
1 tsp paprika,
1/2 tsp cumin,
Salt and pepper to taste,
Olive oil

Samak Harra is a spicy and flavorful fish stew, perfect for spice lovers seeking a taste of the Middle East.

Directions

1. Heat olive oil in a pan. Saute onions and garlic until translucent. Add tomatoes, paprika, cumin, salt, and pepper.
2. Add fish fillet and cook until tender. Serve hot.

Insider Tips

Use any firm white fish for the fillet.

1 serving **35 minutes**

Easy

Bamia (Okra and Tomato Stew)

Ingredients:

1 cup okra (sliced),
1 onion (chopped),
2 tomatoes (diced),
2 cloves garlic (minced),
1 tsp ground coriander,
1/2 tsp cumin,
Salt and pepper to taste,
Olive oil

Bamia is a classic Middle Eastern stew combining tender okra with flavorful tomatoes and aromatic spices.

Directions

1. Heat olive oil in a pan. Saute onions and garlic until fragrant. Add okra and cook until slightly tender.
2. Add tomatoes, coriander, cumin, salt, and pepper. Simmer until okra is cooked.

Insider Tips

Frozen okra can be used as a substitute for fresh okra.

1 serving

90 minutes

Saudi Harees (Wheat and Chicken Porridge)

Normal

Ingredients:

1/2 cup cracked wheat,
1 chicken breast (cut into pieces),
1 onion (chopped),
2 cloves garlic (minced),
1 tsp cinnamon,
Salt to taste,
Water,
Olive oil

Saudi Harees is a comforting porridge made with wheat and chicken, slow-cooked to perfection for a hearty meal.

Directions

1. Heat olive oil in a pot. Saute onions and garlic until golden. Add chicken pieces and brown them.
2. Add cracked wheat, cinnamon, salt, and water. Simmer until thick and creamy.

Insider Tips

Use lamb instead of chicken for a traditional variation.

1 serving   **60 minutes**

Fasolia Khadra Bil Lahme (Green Bean Stew with Meat)

Easy

Ingredients:

1 cup green beans (trimmed),
1/2 lb lamb or beef (cut into cubes),
1 onion (chopped),
2 tomatoes (diced),
2 cloves garlic (minced),
1 tsp cumin,
Salt and pepper to taste,
Olive oil

Fasolia Khadra Bil Lahme is a delicious green bean stew cooked with tender meat and aromatic Middle Eastern spices.

Directions

1. Heat olive oil in a pan. Saute onions and garlic until fragrant. Add meat and brown it.
2. Add green beans, tomatoes, cumin, salt, and pepper. Cook until beans are tender.

Insider Tips

Use canned beans as a quicker alternative to fresh green beans.

Chapter 3:
Grilled Delights

Easy

Shish Tawook (Grilled Chicken Skewers)

Ingredients:

1 lb chicken breast (cut into cubes),
1/2 cup plain yogurt,
2 tbsp olive oil,
4 cloves garlic (minced),
1 tsp paprika,
1 tsp cumin,
1/2 tsp cinnamon,
Salt and pepper to taste

4 servings   20 minutes

Shish Tawook, a Lebanese delight, dances on your taste buds with its marinated chicken perfection. Legend has it that this dish originated in the Lebanese mountains, where locals would marinate chicken in yogurt and spices, creating a succulent harmony of flavors. Its popularity soared as it found its way into Mediterranean cuisine, gracing tables with its juicy tenderness.

Directions

1. In a bowl, mix yogurt, olive oil, garlic, paprika, cumin, cinnamon, salt, and pepper.
2. Add chicken cubes to the marinade, coating evenly. Refrigerate for 1-2 hours.
3. Thread marinated chicken onto skewers.
4. Grill skewers over medium heat until cooked through, about 10-12 minutes, turning occasionally.
5. Serve hot with pita bread and a side of garlic sauce.

Insider Tips

Greek yogurt can replace plain yogurt. Paprika can be substituted with chili powder. Cumin and cinnamon can be found in most spice aisles.

Kofta Kebabs

Ingredients:

1 lb ground lamb or beef,
1/2 onion (finely chopped),
2 cloves garlic (minced),
1/4 cup parsley (chopped),
1 tsp cumin,
1 tsp paprika,
1/2 tsp cinnamon,
Salt and pepper to taste

4 servings   25 minutes

Normal

Kofta Kebabs, hailing from the Middle East, weave a tale of spiced lamb or beef wrapped around skewers, kissed by fire. This dish gained fame as a street food favorite, its aroma beckoning passersby to indulge in its juicy, flavorful bites. Whether served with pita or atop a bed of rice, Kofta Kebabs promise a culinary journey through ancient spice routes.

Directions

1. In a bowl, mix ground meat, onion, garlic, parsley, cumin, paprika, cinnamon, salt, and pepper.
2. Divide mixture into equal portions and shape into elongated kebabs around skewers.
3. Grill kebabs over medium-high heat until cooked through, about 8-10 minutes per side.
4. Serve hot with a side of yogurt sauce and grilled vegetables.

Insider Tips

Ground beef can substitute for lamb. Use cilantro instead of parsley if desired. Paprika and cumin are readily available in stores.

2 servings   15 minutes

Grilled Lamb Chops with Mint Sauce

~~~~~~~~~~~~~~~~~~

Ingredients:

4 lamb chops,
1/4 cup fresh mint leaves (chopped),
2 tbsp olive oil,
2 tbsp lemon juice,
2 cloves garlic (minced),
Salt and pepper to taste

Easy

Grilled Lamb Chops with Mint Sauce transport you to the lush hills of Greece, where tender lamb meets a refreshing mint symphony. This dish's popularity soared as it became a staple at Greek celebrations, symbolizing abundance and togetherness. Served with a side of lemony potatoes, it's a feast fit for the gods.

Directions

1. In a bowl, mix chopped mint, olive oil, lemon juice, garlic, salt, and pepper.
2. Rub lamb chops with the mint mixture, ensuring even coating.
3. Grill chops over medium-high heat until desired doneness, about 3-4 minutes per side for medium-rare.
4. Rest chops before serving and garnish with additional mint leaves.

Insider Tips

Fresh rosemary can replace mint for a different flavor profile. Lemon juice can substitute for vinegar in the mint sauce. Lamb chops can be swapped with beef or pork chops.

Shrimp Kebabs with Garlic Sauce

Easy

4 servings

15 minutes

Ingredients:

1 lb large shrimp (peeled and deveined),
1/4 cup olive oil,
4 cloves garlic (minced),
1 tsp paprika,
1/2 tsp cumin,
1/2 tsp red pepper flakes,
Salt and pepper to taste

Shrimp Kebabs with Garlic Sauce epitomize coastal indulgence, blending succulent seafood with zesty garlic notes. Originating from Mediterranean shores, this dish became a hit at seaside gatherings, its aroma mingling with ocean breezes. Grilled to perfection, each bite is a savory voyage to sun-kissed beaches and culinary bliss.

Directions

1. In a bowl, mix shrimp, olive oil, garlic, paprika, cumin, red pepper flakes, salt, and pepper.
2. Thread shrimp onto skewers.
3. Grill kebabs over medium heat until shrimp are pink and opaque, about 2-3 minutes per side.
4. Serve hot with garlic sauce and a squeeze of lemon.

Insider Tips

Use Cajun seasoning for a spicy twist instead of paprika and cumin. Substitute red pepper flakes with chili powder. Fresh lemon juice can replace garlic sauce. Shrimp can be swapped with cubed chicken or tofu for a different protein option.

4 servings   **30 minutes**

Sumac-Spiced Grilled Vegetables

Ingredients:

2 bell peppers (assorted colors), sliced
1 zucchini, sliced
1 eggplant, sliced
1 red onion, sliced
2 tbsp olive oil
2 tbsp lemon juice
1 tbsp sumac
Salt and pepper to taste

Easy

Sumac-Spiced Grilled Vegetables are a vibrant and flavorful dish, combining a variety of vegetables with a tangy sumac marinade, perfect for summer grilling and adding a pop of color to any meal.

Directions

1. In a bowl, combine olive oil, lemon juice, sumac, salt, and pepper.
2. Toss vegetables in the marinade until coated.
3. Preheat grill and grill vegetables until tender and slightly charred.
4. Serve hot.

Insider Tips

Use any assortment of vegetables like mushrooms, tomatoes, or asparagus.
Replace sumac with lemon zest for a similar citrusy flavor.
Add crushed garlic to the marinade for extra depth.

1 serving

30 minutes

Chicken Shawarma

Ingredients:

1 lb boneless chicken thighs,
1/4 cup plain yogurt,
2 tbsp olive oil,
1 tsp paprika,
Salt & pepper

Easy

Discover the flavors of the Middle East in every bite!

Directions

1. Marinate chicken in yogurt, oil, spices.
2. Grill until cooked.
3. Slice thinly.
4. Serve in pita with tahini, veggies.

Insider Tips

Use Greek yogurt instead of plain yogurt.

1 serving   25 minutes

Spicy Beef Tikka

Ingredients:

1 lb beef chunks,
1/4 cup yogurt,
2 tbsp tomato paste,
1 tsp cumin,
1 tsp chili powder,
Salt & pepper

Normal

A tantalizing blend of spices for meat lovers!

Directions

1. Mix yogurt, spices, marinate beef.
2. Skewer and grill until tender.
3. Serve hot with naan.

Insider Tips

Use chicken or lamb instead of beef.

1 serving

15 minutes

Grilled Halloumi with Honey and Thyme

Ingredients:

6 oz halloumi cheese,
2 tbsp honey,
Fresh thyme leaves,
Olive oil

Super Easy

A savory-sweet delight for cheese enthusiasts!

Directions

1. Slice halloumi, brush with oil, grill until golden.
2. Drizzle honey, garnish with thyme.
3. Serve warm as an appetizer or side dish.

Insider Tips

Use feta cheese if halloumi is unavailable.

1 serving

35 minutes

Swordfish Kebabs

Ingredients:

1 lb swordfish chunks,
1 lemon (juiced),
2 tbsp olive oil,
1 tsp garlic powder,
Salt & pepper

Normal

Dive into the ocean of flavors with these kebabs!

Directions

1. Marinate swordfish in lemon, oil, spices.
2. Skewer and grill until fish flakes.
3. Serve hot with tzatziki sauce.

Insider Tips

Substitute swordfish with tuna or salmon.

1 serving

20 minutes

Kafta Meshwi (Grilled Minced Meat)

Ingredients:

1 lb ground lamb or beef,
1 onion (finely chopped),
2 tbsp parsley (chopped),
1 tsp cumin,
Salt & pepper

Easy

A savory delight straight from the grill!

Directions

1. Mix meat, onion, herbs, spices.
2. Shape into skewers.
3. Grill until cooked.
4. Serve with rice and salad.

Insider Tips

Use ground chicken or turkey for a lighter option.

Chapter 4:
Rice and Pilaf
Paradise

1 servings   **90 minutes**

Normal

Mansaf

~~~~~~~~~~~~~~~~~~~

Ingredients:

1 lb lamb shoulder,
2 cups plain yogurt,
2 cups basmati rice,
1 large onion,
4 cloves garlic,
1/4 cup pine nuts,
2 tbsp clarified butter,
1 tsp ground cardamom,
1 tsp ground cinnamon,
salt and pepper to taste

Mansaf, a Jordanian delight, marries tender lamb with creamy yogurt and fragrant rice in a dish steeped in Bedouin traditions. Legend has it that this dish originated from the nomadic tribes of Jordan, where lamb symbolizes hospitality and generosity.

Directions

1. Marinate lamb in yogurt, cardamom, cinnamon, salt, and pepper.
2. Saute onions and garlic until golden.
3. Add lamb and cook until tender.
4. Toast pine nuts in butter.
5. Cook rice separately.
6. Arrange rice, lamb, and yogurt on a platter.
7. Garnish with pine nuts.

Insider Tips

Use chicken instead of lamb. Substitute Greek yogurt for plain yogurt.

1 servings   **60 minutes**

Normal

Kabsa

Ingredients:

1 lb chicken or lamb,
2 cups basmati rice,
1 large onion,
4 cloves garlic,
2 tomatoes,
1/4 cup raisins,
1/4 cup almonds,
2 tbsp clarified butter,
1 tsp ground cumin,
1 tsp ground coriander,
1 tsp turmeric,
salt and pepper to taste

Kabsa, a Saudi Arabian treasure, weaves aromatic spices with tender meat and fluffy rice for a royal feast fit for kings and queens. Its roots trace back to Bedouin traditions, where every spice tells a story of the Arabian Peninsula's rich culinary heritage.

Directions

1. Saute onions and garlic in butter.
2. Add meat and spices, cook until browned.
3. Add tomatoes, raisins, and almonds.
4. Cook rice separately.
5. Mix rice with meat and serve.

Insider Tips

Use beef instead of chicken or lamb. Substitute dried apricots for raisins.

Normal

1 servings

75 minutes

Maqluba

Ingredients:

1 lb chicken or lamb,
2 cups basmati rice,
1 eggplant,
1 zucchini,
2 tomatoes,
1 large onion,
4 cloves garlic,
1/4 cup almonds,
2 tbsp olive oil,
1 tsp ground turmeric,
1 tsp ground cinnamon,
salt and pepper to taste

Maqluba, an upside-down masterpiece from the Levant, layers fragrant rice, vegetables, and succulent meat to create a culinary marvel. Its name means "upside-down" in Arabic, showcasing the magic of flipping a pot to reveal a stunning dish loved across the Middle East.

Directions

1. Saute onions and garlic, then add meat and spices.
2. Layer vegetables and rice in a pot.
3. Cook until rice is tender.
4. Flip pot to serve.

Insider Tips

Use vegetable broth and omit meat for a vegetarian version. Substitute cauliflower for eggplant.

Maqluba (Upside-Down Rice and Vegetable Dish),37

1 servings   **45 minutes**

Egyptian Kushari

Ingredients:

1 cup lentils,
1 cup rice,
1 cup pasta,
2 large onions,
4 cloves garlic,
2 tomatoes,
1/4 cup vinegar,
2 tbsp olive oil,
1 tsp ground cumin,
1 tsp ground coriander,
salt and pepper to taste

Egyptian Kushari, a street food sensation, combines lentils, rice, pasta, and a tangy tomato sauce for a flavorful and filling dish loved by Egyptians of all walks of life. Its humble origins date back to the 19th century, making it a staple in Egyptian cuisine.

Directions

1. Cook lentils, rice, and pasta separately.
2. Saute onions and garlic, then add tomatoes and spices.
3. Mix everything together and serve with vinegar.

Insider Tips

Use quinoa instead of rice for a healthier option.
Substitute chickpeas for lentils.

1 servings   **60 minutes**

Easy

Persian Jeweled Rice

Ingredients:

2 cups basmati rice,
1/4 cup butter,
1/4 cup dried cranberries,
1/4 cup pistachios,
1/4 cup slivered almonds,
1/4 cup raisins,
1 tsp saffron threads,
1 tsp ground cardamom,
1 tsp ground cinnamon,
salt to taste

Persian Jeweled Rice, a feast for the eyes and palate, embellishes fluffy rice with colorful gems like saffron, dried fruits, and nuts, creating a dish fit for royalty. Its origins date back to ancient Persia, where rice symbolizes prosperity and jewels add a touch of opulence to celebrations.

Directions

1. Cook rice with saffron and spices.
2. Toast nuts and dried fruits separately.
3. Mix everything together and serve.

Insider Tips

Use dried apricots or figs instead of cranberries.
Substitute pine nuts for pistachios.

1 serving　　25 minutes

Easy

Lebanese Rice with Vermicelli

Ingredients:

- 1 cup of long-grain rice
- 1/2 cup of vermicelli
- 2 cups of chicken or vegetable broth
- 1 tablespoon of olive oil
- Salt and pepper to taste
- Optional: chopped parsley for garnish

Lebanese Rice with Vermicelli, a culinary gem from the heart of Lebanon, marries fluffy rice with golden vermicelli strands. A tale of tradition and taste, this dish whispers secrets of spice-laden kitchens, where every grain tells a story of aromatic indulgence.

Directions

1. In a pan, heat olive oil and add vermicelli. Sauté until golden brown.
2. Add rice and sauté for a few minutes.
3. Pour in broth, season with salt and pepper, and bring to a boil.
4. Cover, reduce heat, and simmer until rice is tender.
5. Fluff with a fork, garnish with parsley, and serve hot.

Insider Tips

- Use quinoa for a gluten-free option.
- Replace vermicelli with broken angel hair pasta.

1 serving

60 minutes

Tachin (Saffron Rice Cake with Chicken)

Ingredients:

- 1 cup of basmati rice
- 1/2 cup of yogurt
- 1/4 teaspoon of saffron threads
- 1 tablespoon of butter
- 1 chicken breast (cooked and shredded)
- Salt and pepper to taste

Normal

Tachin, the golden delight of Persian cuisine, weaves a tale of saffron-infused rice encasing tender chicken. A culinary masterpiece, it honors ancient traditions with a modern twist, a symphony of flavors that dances on your palate, leaving a lingering melody of satisfaction.

Directions

1. Rinse rice and soak saffron in warm water.
2. Mix yogurt with saffron water, salt, and pepper.
3. Layer rice in a pan, add yogurt mixture, and top with shredded chicken.
4. Cover with foil and bake until rice is cooked and golden.
5. Invert onto a plate, slice, and serve warm.

Insider Tips

- Use Greek yogurt for a tangy twist.
- Substitute chicken with cooked chickpeas for a vegetarian option.

1 serving   **120 minutes**

Saudi Harees (Savory Wheat and Meat Pudding)

Normal

Ingredients:

- 1 cup of cracked wheat (Harees)
- 1/2 cup of minced meat (beef or lamb)
- 4 cups of water or broth
- 1 onion (chopped)
- 2 cloves of garlic (minced)
- Salt and spices to taste

Saudi Harees, a hearty delight from Saudi Arabia, melds wheat and meat in a comforting embrace. Slow-cooked to perfection, it whispers tales of home kitchens where every spoonful is a hug of warmth, a taste of tradition that soothes the soul.

Directions

1. Rinse cracked wheat and soak for a few hours.
2. In a pot, sauté onion and garlic until golden.
3. Add minced meat, spices, and soaked wheat.
4. Pour in water or broth, bring to a boil, then simmer until thick and creamy.
5. Serve hot, garnished with herbs if desired.

Insider Tips

- Use vegetable broth for a vegetarian version.
- Add vegetables like carrots or peas for extra flavor and nutrition.

1 serving   **40 minutes**

Turkish Pilaf with Pine Nuts and Currants

Easy

Ingredients:

- 1 cup of basmati or long-grain rice
- 2 tablespoons of pine nuts
- 2 tablespoons of currants
- 2 cups of chicken or vegetable broth
- 1 tablespoon of olive oil
- Salt and pepper to taste

Turkish Pilaf with Pine Nuts and Currants, a symphony of flavors from Turkey, blends fluffy rice with crunchy pine nuts and sweet currants. A tribute to culinary finesse, it delights the senses with each spoonful, a journey to the bazaars of Istanbul in every bite.

Directions

1. Toast pine nuts in olive oil until golden.
2. Add rice, currants, and broth. Season with salt and pepper.
3. Bring to a boil, then simmer until rice is tender and liquid is absorbed.
4. Fluff with a fork, sprinkle toasted pine nuts on top, and serve hot.

Insider Tips

- Use almonds or walnuts instead of pine nuts.
- Substitute currants with raisins or dried cranberries.

1 serving   **50 minutes**

Normal

Moroccan Chicken with Preserved Lemon and Olives

mmmmmmmmm

Ingredients:

- 1 chicken leg quarter
- 1 preserved lemon (rinsed and chopped)
- 1/2 cup of green olives
- 1 onion (sliced)
- 2 cloves of garlic (minced)
- Spices (such as cumin, paprika, and cinnamon)
- Olive oil
- Salt and pepper to taste

Moroccan Chicken with Preserved Lemon and Olives, a tapestry of flavors from Morocco, brings together tender chicken with tangy preserved lemons and briny olives. A culinary mosaic, it paints a picture of spice-filled markets and communal feasts, a celebration of taste and togetherness.

Directions

1. Season chicken with spices, salt, and pepper.
2. Sear chicken in olive oil until golden on both sides.
3. Add onions, garlic, preserved lemon, and olives to the pan.
4. Cover and simmer until chicken is cooked through and flavors meld.
5. Serve hot with couscous or crusty bread.

Insider Tips

- Use preserved lemon peel if whole preserved lemons are not available.
- Substitute green olives with black olives or capers.

Chapter 5: Irresistible Sweets

Baklava

Ingredients:

Phyllo dough (16 oz),
melted butter (1 cup),
chopped nuts (3 cups),
sugar (1 cup),
ground cinnamon (1 tsp),
honey (1 cup), water (1 cup),
vanilla extract (1 tsp)

1 piece

45 minutes

Normal

Baklava is a sweet pastry filled with nuts and soaked in honey syrup. This popular dessert originated in the Middle East.

Directions

1. Preheat oven to 350°F.
2. Layer phyllo dough sheets in a baking dish, brushing each layer with melted butter.
3. Mix nuts, sugar, and cinnamon, then sprinkle over the phyllo layers.
4. Bake for 45 minutes until golden brown.
5. Boil honey, water, and vanilla, then pour over the baked baklava.

Insider Tips

Pecans or walnuts can be substituted for other nuts.

1 piece   50 minutes

Normal

Basbousa

Ingredients:

Semolina flour (2 cups),
sugar (1 cup),
plain yogurt (1 cup),
desiccated coconut (1 cup),
baking powder (1 tsp),
melted butter (1/2 cup),
vanilla extract (1 tsp),
blanched almonds (for garnish),
simple syrup (2 cups sugar, 1 cup water, 1 tsp lemon juice)

Basbousa, also known as Semolina Cake, is a moist and flavorful dessert soaked in syrup, popular in Middle Eastern cuisine.

Directions

1. Mix semolina, sugar, yogurt, coconut, baking powder, melted butter, and vanilla.
2. Spread batter in a greased pan, press almond halves on top.
3. Bake at 350°F for 35-40 minutes.
4. Pour cooled syrup over hot cake.
5. Let it cool and absorb syrup before serving.

Insider Tips

Almond flour can be used instead of semolina flour.

1 serving **35 minutes**

Umm Ali

Ingredients:

Puff pastry sheets (1 package),
milk (2 cups),
sugar (1/2 cup),
heavy cream (1/2 cup),
vanilla extract (1 tsp),
chopped nuts (1/2 cup),
raisins (1/4 cup),
shredded coconut (1/4 cup),
ground cinnamon (1 tsp),
butter (2 tbsp),
powdered sugar (for dusting)

Normal

Umm Ali, an Egyptian Bread Pudding, is a rich dessert made with layers of pastry, nuts, and cream, baked to perfection.

Directions

1. Preheat oven to 375°F.
2. Tear puff pastry into pieces, spread in a baking dish.
3. Mix milk, sugar, cream, vanilla, nuts, raisins, coconut, and cinnamon.
4. Pour mixture over pastry, dot with butter.
5. Bake for 25-30 minutes until golden.
6. Dust with powdered sugar before serving.

Insider Tips

Almonds or pistachios can be used instead of other nuts.

2 pieces **30 minutes**

Atayef

Ingredients:

All-purpose flour (2 cups),
semolina (1/2 cup),
sugar (2 tbsp),
yeast (1 tsp),
milk (1 1/2 cups),
water (1/4 cup),
ricotta cheese or chopped nuts (for filling),
simple syrup (1 cup sugar, 1/2 cup water, 1 tsp
lemon juice)

Normal

Atayef, or Stuffed Pancakes, are delicate
pancakes filled with sweet cheese or nuts,
enjoyed during Ramadan in many Middle
Eastern countries.

Directions

1. Mix flour, semolina, sugar, yeast, milk, and
water to make a smooth batter.
2. Let it rest for 15 minutes.
3. Cook small pancakes on one side only.
4. Fill each with cheese or nuts, fold, and seal.
5. Fry until golden brown.
6. Drizzle with warm syrup before serving.

Insider Tips

Cream cheese can be substituted for ricotta
cheese.

Kunafa with Pistachios

1 piece

60 minutes

Normal

Ingredients:

Shredded phyllo dough (1 lb),
unsalted butter (1 cup, melted),
mozzarella cheese (1 lb, shredded),
simple syrup (2 cups sugar,
1 cup water, 1 tsp lemon juice),
chopped pistachios (1/2 cup),
orange blossom water (1 tsp, optional)

Kunafa is a delectable dessert made with shredded phyllo dough, filled with cheese or nuts, and soaked in sugar syrup.

Directions

1. Toss shredded dough with melted butter.
2. Press half of it into a pan as the base.
3. Spread cheese evenly over dough.
4. Cover with remaining dough.
5. Bake at 350°F until golden brown.
6. Pour warm syrup over hot kunafa.
7. Sprinkle pistachios and orange blossom water.

Insider Tips

Ricotta cheese or mixed nuts can be used for filling.

1 dozen   45 minutes

Ma'amoul

Ingredients:

- 1 1/2 cups semolina flour
- 1 1/2 cups all-purpose flour
- 1/2 cup clarified butter
- 1/4 cup powdered sugar
- 1/4 cup milk
- 1/2 teaspoon vanilla extract
- 1 cup pitted dates, chopped
- 1/4 teaspoon ground cinnamon
- Powdered sugar for dusting

Easy

Ma'amoul, a beloved Middle Eastern delicacy, are date-filled cookies traditionally served during festive occasions and celebrations. Their delicate pastry encases a sweet date filling, creating a delightful blend of flavors in every bite.

Directions

1. In a bowl, mix semolina flour, all-purpose flour, clarified butter, powdered sugar, milk, and vanilla extract to form a dough.
2. In a separate bowl, combine chopped dates and ground cinnamon for the filling.
3. Take a small portion of dough, flatten it, and place a teaspoon of date filling in the center. Seal the edges and shape into a ball.
4. Place the cookies on a baking sheet and bake at 350°F (175°C) for 15-20 minutes or until golden brown.
5. Dust with powdered sugar before serving.

Insider Tips

- Substitute clarified butter with unsalted butter
- Use ghee instead of clarified butter
- Replace semolina flour with fine cornmeal
- Replace dates with other dried fruits like figs or apricots

Normal

Rice Pudding with Rose Water

Ingredients:

- 1/2 cup rice
- 4 cups milk
- 1/4 cup sugar
- 1/4 teaspoon ground cardamom
- 1 tablespoon rose water
- Chopped pistachios and rose petals for garnish

This creamy and fragrant rice pudding infused with rose water is a delightful dessert enjoyed in Middle Eastern cuisine. The gentle floral aroma of rose water adds a unique touch to this comforting treat, making it perfect for any occasion.

Directions

1. Rinse the rice and cook it in milk over low heat until soft and creamy, stirring occasionally.
2. Add sugar, ground cardamom, and rose water, stirring until well combined.
3. Continue to cook until the pudding thickens to the desired consistency.
4. Remove from heat and let it cool slightly before serving.
5. Garnish with chopped pistachios and rose petals.

Insider Tips

- Use jasmine or basmati rice
- Replace rose water with orange blossom water
- Add a pinch of saffron for color and flavor

20 pieces   **120 minutes**

Hard

Turkish Delight

Ingredients:

- 1 cup cornstarch
- 1 1/2 cups water
- 2 cups sugar
- 1 tablespoon lemon juice
- 1/4 cup powdered sugar
- Rose water or orange blossom water
- Chopped pistachios for garnish

Turkish Delight, known for its chewy texture and aromatic flavors, is a classic confectionery delight with origins tracing back to the Ottoman Empire. These sweet treats are often infused with rose or orange blossom water and coated in powdered sugar for an extra touch of sweetness.

Directions

1. Mix cornstarch and water in a saucepan over medium heat, stirring until smooth.
2. Add sugar and lemon juice, stirring constantly until the mixture thickens.
3. Remove from heat and stir in rose water or orange blossom water.
4. Pour the mixture into a greased pan and let it set for a few hours.
5. Cut into squares and coat with powdered sugar and chopped pistachios before serving.

Insider Tips

- Use agar-agar instead of cornstarch for a vegan version
- Substitute lemon juice with citric acid
- Customize flavors with different extracts like vanilla or almond

12 pieces

75 minutes

Halawet El-Jibn

Ingredients:

- 1 cup semolina
- 1/2 cup shredded mozzarella cheese
- 1/4 cup sugar
- 1 tablespoon rose water
- 1/4 cup butter
- Chopped pistachios for garnish
- For sugar syrup: 1 cup sugar, 1/2 cup water, 1 tablespoon lemon juice

Halawet El-Jibn, also known as Sweet Cheese Rolls, is a delightful Lebanese dessert made with a creamy cheese filling wrapped in delicate dough and soaked in fragrant sugar syrup. These indulgent rolls are a favorite during Ramadan and special occasions.

Directions

1. Prepare the sugar syrup by boiling sugar, water, and lemon juice until slightly thickened. Set aside to cool.
2. Mix semolina, shredded mozzarella cheese, sugar, and rose water to form a dough.
3. Flatten the dough and place a portion of the cheese mixture in the center. Roll into a log shape.
4. Cut into pieces and bake at 350°F (175°C) until golden brown.
5. Pour the cooled sugar syrup over the warm rolls and garnish with chopped pistachios.

Insider Tips

- Substitute mozzarella with ricotta or cream cheese
- Use vanilla extract instead of rose water
- Drizzle with honey instead of sugar syrup

8 pancakes

60 minutes

Qatayef Asafiri

Ingredients:

For the Pancakes:
1 cup all-purpose flour
1/2 cup semolina
1/4 cup sugar
1 tsp baking powder
1/4 tsp baking soda
1/4 tsp salt
1 cup water
For the Filling:
1 cup ricotta cheese
1/4 cup powdered sugar
1 tsp orange blossom water
1/4 cup crushed pistachios
For Serving:
Honey
Crushed pistachios

Insider Tips

Use mascarpone cheese if ricotta is unavailable. Almonds can be used instead of pistachios.

Qatayef Asafiri, also known as Mini Stuffed Pancakes, is a delightful Middle Eastern dessert that captivates with its delicate texture and luscious filling. Originating from the bustling streets of the Levant, these pancakes are a popular treat during Ramadan and festive occasions. The batter's softness, combined with the richness of the creamy filling, makes every bite a moment of pure indulgence. Get ready to savor the sweetness and warmth of Qatayef Asafiri in every fluffy pancake.

Directions

1. In a bowl, mix flour, semolina, sugar, baking powder, baking soda, and salt.
2. Gradually add water to make a smooth batter.
3. Let the batter rest for 30 minutes.
4. Heat a non-stick pan and pour batter to make small pancakes.
5. Cook until bubbles form, then flip and cook the other side.
6. Mix ricotta, powdered sugar, orange blossom water, and crushed pistachios for the filling.
7. Fill each pancake with the ricotta mixture and fold in half.
8. Drizzle with honey and sprinkle crushed pistachios before serving.

We have a small favor to ask

As we embark on a culinary journey through "The Saudi Arabian Home Cook," we're excited to have you join us for a flavorful exploration of Saudi Arabia's rich culinary heritage!

Now, let's keep it real. We're just passionate cooks, not culinary wizards. If you spot any tiny slip-ups, please forgive us. We're all about learning and improving our kitchen skills!

Your review is the secret ingredient. As a small publisher, your feedback can truly shape the success of our cookbook. Share your thoughts, and let's make this cookbook as delightful as the flavors of Saudi Arabia!

Now, let's get back to cooking up some Middle Eastern delights. It's time to savor the rich heritage of Saudi Arabian cuisine and create delicious memories together!

Warm regards,

Chapter 6:
Bread Bonanza

1 serving   **90 minutes**

Khubz (Arabic Flatbread)

~~~~~~~~~~~~~~~~~~

Ingredients:

3 cups all-purpose flour
1 cup warm water
1 tbsp yeast
1 tsp sugar
1 tsp salt

Normal

Khubz, also known as Arabic flatbread, has been a staple in Middle Eastern cuisine for centuries.
It is a versatile bread that pairs well with various dishes.

Directions

1. Mix yeast, sugar, and warm water. Let it sit for 5 minutes.
2. Combine flour and salt.
3. Knead the dough until smooth.
4. Let it rise for 1 hour.
5. Shape and bake at 475°F for 10-15 minutes.

Insider Tips

Instant yeast for active dry yeast

Easy

Manakish Za'atar

Ingredients:

2 cups all-purpose flour
1 tbsp yeast
1 tsp sugar
1/4 cup olive oil
2 tbsp za'atar spice blend
Salt to taste

Manakish Za'atar is a flavorful flatbread topped with a blend of thyme, sesame seeds, and olive oil.
It's a popular breakfast or snack in the Middle East.

Directions

1. Mix yeast, sugar, and warm water. Let it sit for 5 minutes.
2. Combine flour, salt, and olive oil.
3. Knead the dough until smooth.
4. Let it rise for 30 minutes.
5. Roll out the dough, top with za'atar mix, and bake at 450°F for 10-15 minutes.

Insider Tips

Dried thyme for fresh thyme

Manakish Za'atar (Flatbread with Thyme),59

Easy

1 serving

45 minutes

Markook (Thin Flatbread)

Ingredients:

2 cups all-purpose flour
1 cup warm water
1 tbsp olive oil
1 tsp salt

Markook, also called "Arabic Mountain Bread,"
is a thin, soft bread perfect for wrapping
around grilled meats or dips.
Its simplicity makes it a favorite across the
region.

Directions

1. Mix flour, water, olive oil, and salt until dough forms.
2. Knead until smooth.
3. Divide dough into balls and roll out thinly.
4. Cook on a hot griddle until bubbles form.

Insider Tips

Vegetable oil for olive oil

Normal

Saj Bread

Ingredients:

3 cups all-purpose flour
1 cup warm water
1 tbsp yeast
1 tsp sugar
1 tsp salt
1/4 cup olive oil

1 serving

60 minutes

Saj Bread, cooked on a domed griddle, is a traditional Middle Eastern bread that's soft and chewy.
It's perfect for wrapping around grilled meats or vegetables.

Directions

1. Mix yeast, sugar, and warm water. Let it sit for 5 minutes.
2. Combine flour, salt, and olive oil.
3. Knead until smooth.
4. Let it rise for 30 minutes.
5. Divide and shape dough, then cook on a hot griddle until browned.

Insider Tips

Instant yeast for active dry yeast

Fteer Meshaltet

〰〰〰〰〰〰〰〰〰

Ingredients:

4 cups all-purpose flour
1 cup unsalted butter, melted
1/4 cup vegetable oil
1 tbsp sugar
1 tsp salt

Fteer Meshaltet is a delicate layered pastry with a flaky texture, typically enjoyed with honey or cheese.
Its intricate layers make it a delight to bake and eat.

Directions

1. Mix flour, sugar, and salt. Add melted butter and oil, knead until dough forms.
2. Let it rest for 1 hour.
3. Roll out dough into a thin rectangle.
4. Brush with butter and fold into layers.
5. Bake at 350°F until golden brown.

Insider Tips

Butter for vegetable oil

1 serving

120 minutes

Hard

Normal

8 servings   120 minutes

Barbari Bread

Ingredients:

4 cups bread flour,
1 tbsp active dry yeast,
1 1/2 cups warm water,
1 tsp sugar,
1 tsp salt,
Nigella seeds (optional)

Barbari Bread, a Persian masterpiece, is a chewy yet airy delight that dates back centuries. Legend has it that Persian bakers would hand-stretch this bread, creating its signature texture and flavor. Its popularity grew as it became a staple in Persian cuisine, perfect for scooping up dips or as a side to kebabs. Every bite is a journey through ancient Persian culinary traditions.

Directions

1. Dissolve yeast and sugar in warm water. Let it sit for 5 minutes until frothy.
2. In a large bowl, mix flour and salt. Add yeast mixture and knead until dough forms.
3. Cover and let rise for 1 hour.
4. Divide dough into portions, shape into rectangles.
5. Brush with water and sprinkle nigella seeds.
6. Bake at 400°F for 20-25 minutes.

Insider Tips

Nigella seeds can be omitted. All-purpose flour can substitute for bread flour.

6 servings   90 minutes

Kuboos (Middle Eastern Pita Bread)

Easy

Ingredients:

3 cups all-purpose flour,
1 tbsp yeast,
1 tsp sugar,
1 tsp salt,
1 cup warm water

Kuboos, also known as Middle Eastern Pita Bread, is a soft and versatile bread that has graced tables across the region for generations. Its origin can be traced back to ancient civilizations where it was baked in traditional ovens. Today, it's a staple in Middle Eastern cuisine, perfect for wrapping meats, dips, or enjoying with a drizzle of olive oil.

Directions

1. Mix yeast, sugar, and warm water in a bowl. Let it proof for 5 minutes.
2. In a large bowl, combine flour and salt. Add yeast mixture and knead into a smooth dough.
3. Cover and let rise for 1 hour.
4. Divide dough into balls, roll into circles.
5. Cook on a hot skillet until puffed and lightly browned.
6. Keep warm until serving.

Insider Tips

Bread flour can replace all-purpose flour. Honey can be used instead of sugar.

8 servings   60 minutes

Fatayer Bi Sabanekh (Spinach Pie)

Ingredients:

2 cups flour,
1/2 cup warm water,
1/4 cup olive oil,
1 tsp yeast,
1 tsp sugar,
1 tsp salt,
2 cups chopped spinach,
1 onion (chopped),
1/2 cup pine nuts (toasted),
1/2 cup feta cheese (crumbled),
Sumac and pepper to taste

Normal

Fatayer Bi Sabanekh, or Spinach Pie, is a savory delight that originates from Lebanese kitchens. This pie gained fame for its flaky crust and flavorful spinach filling, seasoned with aromatic herbs. It's a favorite during gatherings, where each slice is a taste of Lebanese hospitality and culinary tradition.

Directions

1. Mix yeast, sugar, and warm water. Let it proof for 5 minutes.
2. In a bowl, combine flour, salt, olive oil, and yeast mixture. Knead into a dough.
3. Cover and let rise for 30 minutes.
4. Mix spinach, onion, pine nuts, feta, sumac, and pepper for filling.
5. Roll out dough, fill with spinach mixture.
6. Bake at 375°F for 20-25 minutes.

Insider Tips

Substitute pine nuts with walnuts or almonds.
Ricotta cheese can replace feta.

Normal

10 servings

120 minutes

Khameer (Sweet Date Bread)

Ingredients:

4 cups flour,
1 cup warm milk,
1/2 cup dates (chopped),
1/4 cup honey,
1/4 cup butter (melted),
1 tbsp yeast,
1 tsp sugar,
1/2 tsp salt,
1/2 tsp ground cardamom

Khameer, a Sweet Date Bread from the Arabian Peninsula, is a soft and aromatic treat that reflects the region's rich culinary heritage. Its origins trace back to Bedouin nomads who crafted this bread using dates for sweetness and warmth. Today, it's enjoyed across the Gulf, often paired with a cup of traditional Arabic coffee. Each bite is a taste of desert tradition.

Directions

1. Mix yeast, sugar, and warm milk. Let it proof for 5 minutes.
2. In a bowl, combine flour, salt, cardamom, dates, honey, and melted butter. Add yeast mixture and knead into a soft dough.
3. Cover and let rise for 1 hour.
4. Shape dough into rounds.
5. Bake at 375°F for 25-30 minutes until golden.

Insider Tips

Use dried figs or raisins if dates are unavailable.
Replace honey with maple syrup.

1 serving **30 minutes**

Easy

A Turkish Delight

Lahmacun

Ingredients:

300g ground lamb
300g ground beef
1 onion, finely chopped
2 tomatoes, diced
2 cloves garlic, minced
2 tbsp tomato paste
2 tbsp olive oil
1 tbsp paprika
1 tsp cumin
1 tsp sumac
Salt and pepper to taste
4-6 round flatbreads
Fresh parsley and lemon wedges for serving

Directions

1. Preheat oven to 220°C (425°F).
2. In a bowl, mix ground meat, onion, tomatoes, garlic, tomato paste, olive oil, paprika, cumin, sumac, salt, and pepper.
3. Divide the mixture evenly and spread it on the flatbreads, leaving a border.
4. Place the Lahmacun on a baking sheet and bake for 10-12 minutes until the edges are crisp and the meat is cooked.
5. Serve hot with fresh parsley and lemon wedges.

Insider Tips

Ground turkey or chicken can be substituted for lamb or beef.
Use store-bought flatbread if homemade is not available.

Chapter 7: Flavorful Dips and Sauces

1 serving   10 minutes

Tahini Sauce

Ingredients:

1/2 cup tahini,
1/4 cup water,
2 tbsp lemon juice,
1 garlic clove (minced),
Salt & pepper

Easy

Dive into the Middle Eastern flavors with this versatile sauce!

Directions

1. Mix tahini, water, lemon juice until smooth.
2. Add garlic, salt, pepper to taste.
3. Adjust consistency with more water if needed.
4. Serve as a dip or drizzle over salads and falafel.

Insider Tips

Use yogurt as a substitute for tahini.

1 serving **15 minutes**

Toum (Garlic Sauce)

Ingredients:

1 cup garlic cloves,
1 cup vegetable oil,
1/4 cup lemon juice,
Salt

Normal

This garlic-packed sauce adds a punch to any dish!

Directions

1. Blend garlic, lemon juice until smooth.
2. Gradually add oil until emulsified.
3. Season with salt.
4. Store in airtight container.
5. Use as a dip for grilled meats or spread on sandwiches.

Insider Tips

Use mayonnaise instead of vegetable oil for a creamier texture.

Easy

1 serving

5 minutes

Zhug (Yemeni Hot Sauce)

Ingredients:

1/2 cup cilantro,
1/4 cup parsley,
2-3 green chilies,
2 garlic cloves,
1 tsp cumin,
Salt

Feel the heat with this spicy Yemeni sauce!

Directions

1. Blend all ingredients until smooth.
2. Adjust seasoning to taste.
3. Add a dash of olive oil if desired.
4. Serve as a condiment for grilled meats or as a dip with bread.

Insider Tips

Use jalapeños or serrano peppers instead of green chilies.

Amba (Pickled Mango Sauce)

1 serving

20 minutes

Normal

Ingredients:

1 ripe mango (peeled, diced),
1/4 cup vinegar,
1/4 cup sugar,
1 tsp turmeric,
1/2 tsp cumin,
Salt & pepper

Tangy and flavorful, this sauce adds a tropical twist to your meals!

Directions

1. Cook mango, vinegar, sugar until mango softens.
2. Add turmeric, cumin, salt, pepper.
3. Simmer until thickened.
4. Cool before serving.
5. Use as a topping for grilled fish or as a dip.

Insider Tips

Use canned mango pulp if fresh mango is not available.

1 serving

10 minutes

Tarator (Sesame Seed Sauce)

Ingredients:

1/2 cup sesame seeds,
1/4 cup water,
2 tbsp lemon juice,
1 garlic clove,
Salt & pepper

A creamy sauce with a nutty flavor, perfect for salads or grilled veggies!

Directions

1. Toast sesame seeds until golden.
2. Blend with water, lemon juice, garlic until smooth.
3. Season with salt, pepper.
4. Adjust consistency with more water if needed.
5. Serve as a dressing.

Insider Tips

Use almond or cashew butter instead of sesame seeds for a nut-free version.

1 servings   10 minutes

Easy

Pomegranate Molasses Dressing

Ingredients:

1/4 cup pomegranate molasses,
1/4 cup olive oil,
2 tbsp lemon juice,
1 tsp Dijon mustard,
1 clove garlic (minced),
salt and pepper to taste

Pomegranate Molasses Dressing adds a tangy-sweet twist to salads, inspired by the Middle Eastern culinary tradition of using pomegranates for their vibrant flavor and health benefits. This dressing is a delightful fusion of tartness and richness.

Directions

1. Whisk together pomegranate molasses, olive oil, lemon juice, mustard, garlic, salt, and pepper.
2. Adjust seasoning to taste.

Insider Tips

Use balsamic vinegar instead of pomegranate molasses.

Muhammara Sauce

~~~~~~~~~~~~~~~~~~~~

Ingredients:

2 roasted red peppers,
1/2 cup walnuts,
2 tbsp olive oil,
1 tbsp pomegranate molasses,
1 tbsp lemon juice,
1 clove garlic,
1 tsp ground cumin,
1/2 tsp smoked paprika,
salt and pepper to taste

Easy

1 servings   15 minutes

Muhammara Sauce, a beloved Syrian dip, blends roasted red peppers, walnuts, and spices into a creamy texture bursting with flavor. Its origins trace back to Aleppo, where it has been cherished for centuries as a symbol of hospitality and culinary excellence.

Directions

1. Blend red peppers, walnuts, olive oil, pomegranate molasses, lemon juice, garlic, cumin, paprika, salt, and pepper until smooth.
2. Adjust seasoning to taste.
3. Drizzle with olive oil before serving.

Insider Tips

Use almonds instead of walnuts. Substitute honey for pomegranate molasses.

1 servings   5 minutes

Yogurt and Cucumber Sauce

Ingredients:

1/2 cup Greek yogurt,
1/2 cucumber (peeled and grated),
1 tbsp fresh mint (chopped),
1 clove garlic (minced),
1 tbsp lemon juice,
salt and pepper to taste

Easy

Yogurt and Cucumber Sauce, a refreshing accompaniment to Middle Eastern dishes, combines cool yogurt with crisp cucumbers and a hint of mint. Its simplicity and versatility make it a staple in Mediterranean cuisine, adding a creamy and tangy element to meals.

Directions

1. Mix together yogurt, cucumber, mint, garlic, lemon juice, salt, and pepper.
2. Adjust seasoning to taste.

Insider Tips

Use dill instead of mint. Substitute lime juice for lemon juice.

1 servings   **5 minutes**

Easy

Sumac Yogurt

Ingredients:

1/2 cup Greek yogurt,
1 tbsp sumac,
1 tbsp olive oil,
1 clove garlic (minced),
salt and pepper to taste

Sumac Yogurt, a tangy and aromatic sauce, elevates dishes with its distinctive flavor from the Middle East. Sumac adds a citrusy punch to creamy yogurt, perfect for drizzling over grilled meats or as a dip for bread.

Directions

1. Mix together yogurt, sumac, olive oil, garlic, salt, and pepper.
2. Adjust seasoning to taste.

Insider Tips

Use lemon zest instead of sumac. Substitute minced shallots for garlic.

Date Syrup Drizzle

1 servings   5 minutes

Easy

Ingredients:

1/4 cup date syrup,
1 tbsp lemon juice,
1/2 tsp ground cinnamon,
pinch of salt

Date Syrup Drizzle adds a natural sweetness to dishes, inspired by the rich flavors of the Middle East. Date syrup, known for its deep caramel notes, complements both sweet and savory dishes, creating a delightful finishing touch.

Directions

1. Whisk together date syrup, lemon juice, cinnamon, and salt until combined.
2. Drizzle over desserts or savory dishes as desired.

Insider Tips

Use maple syrup or honey instead of date syrup.

Chapter 8: Arabian Delights from the Sea

1 serving   **25 minutes**

Grilled Fish with Tarator Sauce

Normal

Ingredients:

1 fish fillet,
2 tbsp tahini,
1 tbsp lemon juice,
1 clove garlic (minced),
1 tbsp chopped parsley,
Salt and pepper to taste

Originating from Lebanon, this dish features tender grilled fish topped with a tangy tarator sauce made from tahini, lemon juice, garlic, and parsley.

Directions

1. Preheat grill to medium-high heat.
2. Season fish with salt and pepper.
3. Grill fish for 4-5 minutes per side until cooked through.

Insider Tips

Tahini can be replaced with Greek yogurt for a creamier sauce.

Grilled Fish with Tarator Sauce,80

Sayadieh (Lebanese Fish Pilaf)

Ingredients:

1 cup basmati rice,
1 fish fillet,
1 onion (sliced),
1 tsp cumin,
1 tsp paprika,
Salt and pepper to taste

Normal

Sayadieh is a classic Lebanese dish featuring seasoned rice cooked with fish, caramelized onions, and a blend of aromatic spices.

Directions

1. Cook rice according to package instructions.
2. Sauté onions until caramelized.
3. Season fish with cumin, paprika, salt, and pepper.
4. Cook fish until done.

Insider Tips

Use any white fish like cod or tilapia as a substitute for the fish fillet.

1 serving   **50 minutes**

Shrimp Biryani

Ingredients:

1 cup basmati rice, 8-10 shrimp (peeled and deveined),
1 onion (sliced),
2 tbsp biryani masala,
1/2 cup yogurt,
Salt to taste

Normal

Aromatic and flavorful, Shrimp Biryani is a cherished Indian dish with layers of spiced shrimp, fragrant rice, and caramelized onions.

Directions

1. Cook rice until almost done.
2. Sauté onions until golden brown.
3. Marinate shrimp in biryani masala and yogurt.
4. Layer rice, shrimp, and onions.
5. Cook until shrimp is cooked through.

Insider Tips

Use chicken or vegetables instead of shrimp for a different variation.

1 serving   **60 minutes**

Normal

Ouzi (Stuffed Baked Fish)

Ingredients:

1 fish (whole, cleaned),
1/2 cup cooked rice,
2 tbsp chopped nuts,
2 tbsp raisins,
1 tsp cinnamon,
Salt and pepper to taste

Ouzi is a Middle Eastern delight, featuring baked fish stuffed with a flavorful mixture of rice, nuts, raisins, and spices.

Directions

1. Preheat oven to 375°F.
2. Mix cooked rice, nuts, raisins, cinnamon, salt, and pepper.
3. Stuff fish with mixture.
4. Bake until fish is cooked through.

Insider Tips

Use quinoa or couscous instead of rice for a gluten-free option.

1 serving   **40 minutes**

Normal

Fish Tagine with Chermoula

Ingredients:

1 fish fillet,
1/2 cup chermoula sauce,
1/4 cup olives,
2 tbsp preserved lemon (chopped),
Salt and pepper to taste

A Moroccan specialty, Fish Tagine with Chermoula combines tender fish cooked in a savory chermoula sauce with olives and preserved lemons.

Directions

1. Season fish with salt and pepper.
2. Spread chermoula sauce on fish.
3. Top with olives and preserved lemon.
4. Bake until fish is cooked.

Insider Tips

Use any firm white fish like halibut or sea bass for this dish.

1 serving

30 minutes

Normal

Seafood Couscous

~~~~~~~~~~~~~~~~~~~~~~~~~~~~~~

Ingredients:

1 cup couscous
200g mixed seafood
1 onion, diced
1 bell pepper, diced
2 tomatoes, chopped
1 tsp cumin
1 tsp paprika
Salt and pepper to taste

A flavorful Moroccan dish blending couscous with a medley of seafood, infused with aromatic spices and herbs.

Directions

1. Cook couscous according to package instructions.
2. In a pan, sauté onions and bell pepper until soft.
3. Add tomatoes, spices, and seafood. Cook until seafood is done.
4. Serve seafood mixture over couscous.

Insider Tips

Use any seafood of your choice.

Egyptian Fish Balls

Ingredients:

200g white fish fillets
1 onion, grated
2 garlic cloves, minced
1 tsp cumin
1 tsp coriander
Salt and pepper to taste
Oil for frying

Traditional Egyptian fish balls made with a blend of spices and herbs, fried to crispy perfection and served with a tangy dipping sauce.

Directions

1. Blend fish, onion, garlic, spices, salt, and pepper in a food processor.
2. Form mixture into balls.
3. Fry fish balls until golden brown.
4. Serve hot with dipping sauce.

Insider Tips

Serve with tahini sauce or aioli.

1 serving **20 minutes**

Spicy Crab Salad

Ingredients:

200g crab meat
1 cucumber, diced
1 tomato, diced
1/2 red onion, thinly sliced
1/2 red chili, minced
2 tbsp olive oil
1 tbsp lemon juice
Salt and pepper to taste

Easy

A refreshing salad featuring tender crab meat tossed with crisp vegetables and a spicy dressing, perfect for a light meal.

Directions

1. Mix crab meat, cucumber, tomato, onion, and chili in a bowl.
2. In a separate bowl, whisk olive oil, lemon juice, salt, and pepper for the dressing.
3. Pour dressing over the salad and toss gently.
4. Serve chilled.

Insider Tips

Use shrimp or cooked chicken instead of crab.

Normal

1 serving

35 minutes

Moroccan Fish Kofta

Ingredients:

200g white fish fillets
1 onion, finely chopped
2 garlic cloves, minced
1 tbsp cilantro, chopped
1 tsp cumin
1 tsp paprika
Salt and pepper to taste
1/4 cup plain yogurt
1 tbsp lemon juice

Spiced fish koftas infused with Moroccan flavors, grilled to perfection and served with a zesty yogurt sauce.

Directions

1. In a bowl, mix fish, onion, garlic, cilantro, spices, salt, and pepper. Form into kofta shapes.
2. Grill koftas until cooked through.
3. Mix yogurt, lemon juice, salt, and pepper for the sauce.
4. Serve koftas with yogurt sauce.

Insider Tips

Use ground chicken or turkey instead of fish.

Normal

1 serving

45 minutes

Bahraini Spiced Prawn Soup

Ingredients:

200g prawns, peeled and deveined
1 onion, chopped
2 tomatoes, chopped
1 carrot, diced
1 potato, diced
2 cups vegetable broth
1 tsp baharat spice mix
Salt and pepper to taste

A comforting and aromatic soup featuring succulent prawns simmered in a flavorful broth with Bahraini spices and vegetables.

Directions

1. In a pot, sauté onion until translucent. Add tomatoes, carrot, potato, baharat spice mix, salt, and pepper.
2. Pour in vegetable broth and simmer until vegetables are tender.
3. Add prawns and cook until done.
4. Serve hot.

Insider Tips

Use chicken or vegetable broth if preferred.

Chapter 9: Vegetarian Wonders

4 servings   45 minutes

Easy

Mujadara

~~~~~~~~~~~~~~~~~~

Ingredients:

- 1 cup brown lentils
- 1/2 cup rice
- 2 onions, thinly sliced
- 3 tablespoons olive oil
- 1 teaspoon cumin
- Salt and pepper to taste
- Chopped parsley for garnish

Mujadara, a comforting Middle Eastern dish, combines lentils and rice with caramelized onions for a flavorful and nutritious meal. This dish has roots in ancient Arab cuisine and is loved for its simplicity and rich taste.

Directions

1. Rinse lentils and rice, then cook them separately until tender.
2. In a pan, caramelize onions in olive oil until golden brown.
3. Add cumin, salt, and pepper to the onions.
4. Mix lentils, rice, and half of the caramelized onions in a serving dish.
5. Top with the remaining onions and chopped parsley before serving.

Insider Tips

- Use white rice instead of brown
- Substitute cumin with coriander
- Add garlic for extra flavor
- Garnish with toasted pine nuts or almonds

4 servings **60 minutes**

Stuffed Bell Peppers with Couscous

Ingredients:

- 4 bell peppers, halved and deseeded
- 1 cup couscous
- 1 onion, diced
- 1 zucchini, diced
- 1 carrot, grated
- 1 teaspoon paprika
- Salt and pepper to taste
- Olive oil for cooking
- Grated cheese for topping

Insider Tips

- Substitute couscous with quinoa or bulgur
- Use any color bell peppers
- Add chopped herbs like parsley or cilantro to the filling

Normal

Stuffed bell peppers filled with couscous, vegetables, and spices create a vibrant and satisfying dish. Originating from Mediterranean cuisine, this recipe offers a delightful blend of flavors and textures in every bite.

Directions

1. Cook couscous according to package instructions and set aside.
2. In a pan, sauté onion, zucchini, and carrot in olive oil until tender.
3. Add paprika, salt, and pepper to the vegetables.
4. Mix cooked couscous with the vegetable mixture.
5. Stuff the bell pepper halves with the couscous filling.
6. Top with grated cheese and bake at 375°F (190°C) for 20-25 minutes or until peppers are tender.
7. Serve hot.

4 servings   **45 minutes**

Easy

Egyptian Molokhia

Ingredients:

- 1 bunch molokhia leaves
- 4 cups chicken or vegetable broth
- 4 cloves garlic, minced
- 2 tablespoons olive oil
- Salt and pepper to taste
- Lemon wedges for serving

Molokhia, a traditional Egyptian dish, features a flavorful stew made with jute leaves, garlic, and spices. This nutritious dish is often served with rice or bread and is beloved for its unique taste and cultural significance.

Directions

1. Wash molokhia leaves thoroughly and chop finely.
2. In a pot, heat olive oil and sauté minced garlic until golden.
3. Add molokhia leaves and sauté for a few minutes.
4. Pour in chicken or vegetable broth and simmer until the leaves are tender.
5. Season with salt and pepper to taste.
6. Serve hot with a squeeze of lemon juice.

Insider Tips

- Substitute molokhia leaves with spinach
- Use beef or lamb broth for a richer flavor
- Add chopped onions and tomatoes for extra texture

4 servings **60 minutes**

Imam Bayildi

Ingredients:

- 2 large eggplants
- 2 tomatoes, diced
- 1 onion, diced
- 3 cloves garlic, minced
- 1/4 cup chopped parsley
- 2 tablespoons olive oil
- Salt and pepper to taste

Normal

Imam Bayildi, a classic Turkish dish, features eggplants stuffed with a flavorful mixture of tomatoes, onions, and herbs. Legend has it that the imam fainted upon tasting this dish due to its exquisite taste, hence the name "Imam Bayildi," which means "the imam fainted."

Directions

1. Cut eggplants in half lengthwise and scoop out the flesh, leaving a shell.
2. Sauté onion and garlic in olive oil until translucent.
3. Add diced tomatoes, chopped eggplant flesh, parsley, salt, and pepper to the pan.
4. Cook until the mixture is soft and fragrant.
5. Stuff the eggplant shells with the mixture.
6. Place stuffed eggplants in a baking dish, drizzle with olive oil, and bake at 375°F (190°C) for 30-35 minutes.
7. Serve hot or at room temperature.

Insider Tips

- Add pine nuts or raisins to the stuffing
- Use bell peppers instead of eggplants
- Garnish with crumbled feta cheese

Normal

Musakhan Rolls

Ingredients:

- 1 pound boneless chicken thighs, cooked and shredded
- 1 onion, thinly sliced
- 1 tablespoon sumac
- 1/4 cup pine nuts, toasted
- 6 large flatbreads or tortillas
- Olive oil for brushing
- Salt and pepper to taste
- Chopped parsley for garnish

Musakhan Rolls, inspired by Palestinian cuisine, are sumac-spiced rolls filled with roasted chicken, onions, and pine nuts. This dish is a celebration of traditional flavors and is often served at festive gatherings and family meals.

Directions

1. Mix shredded chicken with sumac, salt, and pepper.
2. Sauté sliced onions until caramelized, then add to the chicken mixture.
3. Divide the chicken and onion mixture among the flatbreads, sprinkle with toasted pine nuts, and roll into tight cylinders.
4. Brush the rolls with olive oil and bake at 375°F (190°C) for 10-15 minutes or until golden and crispy.
5. Garnish with chopped parsley before serving.

Insider Tips

- Use rotisserie chicken for convenience
- Substitute sumac with a blend of paprika and lemon zest
- Add a drizzle of tahini or yogurt sauce inside the rolls

4 servings   **60 minutes**

Normal

Fava Bean Stew

Ingredients:

2 cups dried fava beans,
1 onion,
2 carrots,
2 tomatoes,
2 cloves garlic,
vegetable broth,
cumin,
paprika,
salt,
pepper,
olive oil

Hearty Comfort
Fava Bean Stew is a hearty and comforting dish with origins in Mediterranean cuisine. This stew combines tender fava beans, vegetables, and aromatic spices for a flavorful and nutritious meal.
Indulge in the comforting flavors of Fava Bean Stew and experience the warmth of homemade goodness.

Directions

1. Soak fava beans overnight and drain.
2. Sauté chopped onions, carrots, and garlic in olive oil until soft.
3. Add soaked fava beans, chopped tomatoes, vegetable broth, and spices.
4. Simmer for 45 minutes or until beans are tender.
5. Adjust seasoning if needed and serve hot.

Insider Tips

Fava beans - Lima beans, Vegetable broth - Chicken broth

Lebanese Lentil Salad

mmmmmmm

Ingredients:

1 cup lentils,
cucumber,
tomatoes,
red onion,
parsley,
mint,
lemon juice,
olive oil,
garlic,
salt,
pepper

4 servings

30 minutes

Easy

Zesty Delight
Lebanese Lentil Salad is a zesty delight that
combines lentils, fresh vegetables, and herbs with a
tangy dressing. This salad is a staple in Lebanese
cuisine, known for its vibrant flavors and nutritious
ingredients.
Enjoy the zesty freshness of Lebanese Lentil Salad
and add a burst of flavor to your meal.

Directions

1. Cook lentils until tender, then drain and cool.
2. Chop cucumbers, tomatoes, red onion,
parsley, and mint.
3. Mix lentils and vegetables in a bowl.
4. In a separate bowl, whisk lemon juice, olive
oil, minced garlic, salt, and pepper to make the
dressing.
5. Pour dressing over salad and toss to
combine.
6. Serve chilled.

Insider Tips

Lentils - Chickpeas, Mint - Cilantro

4 servings   **45 minutes**

Normal

Okra and Chickpea Tagine

Ingredients:

1 lb okra,
1 can chickpeas,
2 tomatoes,
onion,
garlic,
ginger,
cumin,
coriander,
paprika,
cinnamon,
salt,
pepper,
olive oil

Exotic Fusion
Okra and Chickpea Tagine is an exotic fusion of flavors inspired by Moroccan cuisine. This tagine combines tender okra, chickpeas, tomatoes, and fragrant spices for a delicious and aromatic stew. Experience the exotic fusion of Okra and Chickpea Tagine and transport your taste buds to the enchanting world of Moroccan cuisine.

Directions

1. Sauté chopped onions, garlic, and ginger in olive oil until golden.
2. Add chopped tomatoes and spices, cook until tomatoes soften.
3. Add sliced okra, chickpeas, and a little water.
4. Simmer until okra is tender.
5. Adjust seasoning if needed and serve hot with couscous or bread.

Insider Tips

Okra - Green beans, Chickpeas - White beans

6 servings

60 minutes

Spinach and Feta Börek

Ingredients:

1 package phyllo dough,
1 lb spinach,
feta cheese,
onions,
garlic,
dill,
olive oil,
salt, pepper

Savory Delight
Spinach and Feta Börek is a savory delight from Turkish cuisine, featuring layers of crispy phyllo pastry filled with spinach, feta cheese, and herbs. This dish is a favorite for breakfast, brunch, or as a snack.
Enjoy the savory goodness of Spinach and Feta Börek and delight your taste buds with its flaky and flavorful layers.

Directions

1. Sauté chopped onions and garlic in olive oil until translucent.
2. Add chopped spinach and cook until wilted.
3. Season with salt, pepper, and dill.
4. Layer phyllo dough sheets in a baking dish, brushing each layer with olive oil.
5. Spread spinach mixture and crumbled feta between layers.
6. Bake until golden and crispy.
7. Let cool slightly before slicing and serving.

Insider Tips

Phyllo dough - Puff pastry, Feta cheese - Ricotta cheese

Chapter 10: Exotic Beverages

4 servings   10 minutes

Mint Lemonade

Ingredients:

1/2 cup fresh lemon juice
1/2 cup sugar
1/4 cup fresh mint leaves
4 cups cold water
Ice cubes
Lemon slices for garnish

Mint Lemonade is a cool and refreshing drink perfect for hot summer days, blending tangy lemon juice with fresh mint leaves for a burst of flavor.

Directions

1. In a pitcher, combine lemon juice, sugar, and mint leaves. Stir until sugar dissolves.
2. Add cold water and stir.
3. Serve over ice with lemon slices.

Insider Tips

Replace sugar with honey for a healthier option.
Add a splash of sparkling water for fizz.
Use lime juice instead of lemon for a different twist.

Normal

4 servings   20 minutes

Tamarind Juice

~~~~~~~~~~~~~~~~~~~

Ingredients:

1/2 cup tamarind pulp
1/2 cup sugar
4 cups water
Ice cubes
Mint leaves for garnish

Tamarind Juice is a tangy and sweet drink made from tamarind pulp, sugar, and water, offering a unique and refreshing flavor profile.

Directions

1. In a bowl, soak tamarind pulp in water for 15 minutes, then strain to remove seeds.
2. Add sugar to tamarind water and stir until dissolved.
3. Serve chilled with ice cubes and mint leaves.

Insider Tips

Use tamarind concentrate for convenience.
Replace sugar with agave syrup for a healthier option.
Add a pinch of salt for balance.

Jallab (Date and Grape Molasses Drink)

Ingredients:

1/2 cup date syrup
2 tbsp grape molasses
1 tbsp rose water
4 cups cold water
Ice cubes
Pine nuts and raisins for garnish

Easy

Jallab is a popular Middle Eastern drink made from date syrup, grape molasses, and rose water, creating a sweet and aromatic beverage.

Directions

1. In a pitcher, combine date syrup, grape molasses, rose water, and cold water. Stir well.
2. Serve over ice and garnish with pine nuts and raisins.

Insider Tips

Replace rose water with orange blossom water for a floral twist.
Add a sprinkle of ground cinnamon for extra flavor.
Use maple syrup if date syrup is unavailable.

4 servings   **30 minutes**

Normal

Qamar al-Din (Apricot Juice)

Ingredients:

4 sheets dried apricots
1/2 cup sugar
4 cups water
Ice cubes
Lemon slices for garnish

Qamar al-Din is a traditional Middle Eastern drink made from dried apricot sheets, sugar, and water, known for its rich and fruity taste.

Directions

1. Soak dried apricot sheets in water for several hours or overnight until softened.
2. Blend apricot sheets with sugar and water until smooth.
3. Serve chilled over ice with lemon slices.

Insider Tips

Use fresh apricots if dried sheets are not available.
Add a splash of orange juice for extra citrusy flavor.
Adjust sugar according to sweetness preference.

1 serving

10 minutes

Turkish Coffee

Ingredients:

1 tbsp finely ground Turkish coffee
1 cup water
Sugar to taste
Cardamom (optional)

Turkish Coffee is a strong and aromatic coffee brewed with finely ground coffee beans and served in small cups, offering a rich and intense coffee experience.

Directions

1. In a cezve (Turkish coffee pot), combine coffee, water, and sugar. Stir well.
2. Heat over low flame until it starts to foam.
3. Pour into cups, including the foam. Add cardamom if desired.

Insider Tips

Use espresso coffee for a similar strong flavor.
Add a cinnamon stick for extra spice.
Serve with a glass of water to cleanse the palate.

Kashmiri Chai

Normal

2 servings   45 minutes

munummununu

Ingredients:

2 cups water
2 cups whole milk
2 tbsp loose black tea
4 green cardamom pods
4 cloves
1-inch cinnamon stick
1/2 tsp fennel seeds
1/4 tsp saffron strands
1/4 cup sugar
Chopped almonds and pistachios for garnish

Kashmiri Chai is a beloved beverage originating from the scenic valleys of Kashmir, known for its rich flavor and vibrant hue. This pink-hued tea is infused with a blend of aromatic spices and enriched with creamy milk, creating a delightful drink that warms the soul. Whether enjoyed during chilly evenings or as a comforting treat, Kashmiri Chai brings a touch of tradition and warmth to every sip. Get ready to savor the exotic flavors of Kashmir in this enchanting tea.

Directions

1. In a pot, bring water to a boil with cardamom, cloves, cinnamon, fennel seeds, and saffron.
2. Add loose tea and simmer for 5 minutes.
3. Add milk and sugar, simmer for another 10 minutes.
4. Strain and serve hot, garnished with chopped almonds and pistachios.

Insider Tips

Use almond milk for a dairy-free version.
Adjust sugar according to taste preferences.

1 serving

5 minutes

Ayran (Yogurt Drink)

Ingredients:

1 cup plain yogurt
1/2 cup cold water
Pinch of salt
Fresh mint leaves for garnish

Super Easy

Ayran is a refreshing yogurt-based drink popular in Middle Eastern and Mediterranean cuisines, known for its cooling properties and tangy flavor. Originating from Turkey, this simple yet satisfying drink combines yogurt, water, and a pinch of salt to create a thirst-quenching beverage perfect for hot days. Whether enjoyed as a standalone refreshment or paired with spicy dishes, Ayran is a beloved companion to any meal. Get ready to experience the invigorating taste of Ayran in every sip.

Directions

1. In a blender, combine yogurt, water, and salt. Blend until smooth and frothy.
2. Pour into a glass over ice.
3. Garnish with fresh mint leaves before serving.

Insider Tips

Add a squeeze of lemon juice for extra tanginess.
Use Greek yogurt for a creamier texture.

2 servings   15 minutes

Easy

Qishr (Yemeni Spiced Coffee)

Ingredients:

2 cups water
2 tbsp dried coffee cherries
2 cardamom pods
2 cloves
1-inch cinnamon stick
1/4 tsp ground ginger
1/4 tsp ground nutmeg
Sugar or honey to taste
Optional: pinch of saffron

Qishr is a traditional Yemeni beverage made from dried coffee cherries, infused with aromatic spices for a unique and invigorating flavor. This spiced coffee is a cultural delight, enjoyed for its warming properties and distinctive taste. Originating from the ancient coffee traditions of Yemen, Qishr is a beloved drink that brings together the rich heritage of coffee with the allure of exotic spices. Get ready to embark on a sensory journey with every sip of Qishr, capturing the essence of Yemeni hospitality and tradition.

Directions

1. In a pot, bring water to a boil with coffee cherries, cardamom, cloves, cinnamon, ginger, nutmeg, and saffron (if using).
2. Simmer for 10 minutes.
3. Strain into cups, sweeten with sugar or honey as desired.
4. Serve hot and enjoy the aromatic flavors of Qishr.

Insider Tips

Use ground coffee if dried coffee cherries are unavailable.
Adjust spices and sweetness according to taste preferences.

1 serving   **10 minutes**

Rose Water and Cardamom Milk

Ingredients:

1 cup milk
1/4 tsp rose water
1/4 tsp ground cardamom
1 tbsp honey or sugar (optional)

Easy

Rose Water and Cardamom Milk is a fragrant and soothing drink infused with the floral notes of rose water and the warm spice of cardamom. Originating from the aromatic kitchens of the Middle East, this milk-based beverage is known for its calming properties and delightful flavor. Whether enjoyed as a bedtime treat or a relaxing afternoon drink, Rose Water and Cardamom Milk offers a moment of tranquility with every sip. Get ready to unwind and indulge in the gentle aromas of roses and cardamom in this enchanting drink.

Directions

1. In a small saucepan, heat milk over low heat.
2. Add rose water, ground cardamom, and sweetener if using.
3. Stir until warmed through and fragrant.
4. Pour into a cup and enjoy warm.

Insider Tips

Use almond milk or oat milk for a dairy-free version.
Adjust sweetness according to taste preferences.

1 serving **10 minutes**

Saffron Tea

Ingredients:

1 cup water
Pinch of saffron threads
1 tsp honey or sugar (optional)

Easy

Saffron Tea is a luxurious and aromatic beverage that showcases the delicate flavors of saffron, prized for its exotic essence and golden hue. Originating from ancient Persia, this tea is a symbol of elegance and refinement, often enjoyed during special occasions. Infused with the subtle sweetness of saffron, this tea offers a sensory experience like no other, inviting you to savor the richness of this precious spice. Get ready to indulge in the opulence of Saffron Tea and elevate your tea-drinking experience to new heights.

Directions

1. In a saucepan, bring water to a boil.
2. Add saffron threads and simmer for 5 minutes.
3. Sweeten with honey or sugar if desired.
4. Pour into a cup and enjoy the aromatic flavors of Saffron Tea.

Insider Tips

Add a dash of ground cardamom for extra flavor.
Adjust sweetness according to taste preferences.

We have a small favor to ask

As we approach the final pages of "The Saudi Arabian Home Cook: Taste Saudi Arabia's Rich Heritage - A Middle Eastern Cookbook with 100+ Recipes and Stunning Pictures," we extend a warm invitation to you.

Crafting this culinary masterpiece has been a journey through the rich tapestry of flavors and traditions of Saudi Arabia. Each recipe is a tribute to the vibrant culinary heritage of the Middle East, carefully crafted to bring the essence of Saudi Arabian cuisine into your home.

Yet, even the most meticulously crafted dishes can benefit from feedback. If you encounter any flavors or techniques that don't quite meet your expectations, please accept our humble apologies. We are committed to continuous improvement and value your honest thoughts and suggestions.

Your review is essential to us as a small publisher. Your participation shapes the future of our culinary endeavors, guiding us in refining our recipes and sharing the rich heritage of Saudi Arabian cuisine with more readers.

As you explore "The Saudi Arabian Home Cook," we invite you to savor not only the flavors but also the stories and traditions woven into each dish. And while you're here, why not discover more culinary treasures waiting to be unearthed under the Garden of Grapes?

Thank you for being a part of our culinary journey. Your support and feedback mean the world to us.

Warm regards,

BONUS

In this moment, we're excited to introduce 10 additional bonus recipes from the Garden of Grapes. Be adventurous and try something new that you might enjoy!

Smoked Pork Belly Burnt Ends

Serving Size: 4-6 servings/ Prep Time: 6 hours/ Cal: 450 calories per serving

Ingredients:

2 lbs pork belly
2 tbsp kosher salt
2 tbsp black pepper
2 tbsp garlic powder
2 tbsp onion powder
2 tbsp paprika
2 tbsp brown sugar
1 cup BBQ sauce

Insider Tips

For extra tenderness, you can wrap the pork belly in foil during the last hour of cooking. Also, make sure to use a meat thermometer to ensure the pork is fully cooked.

Pork belly burnt ends are a delicious and indulgent smoked dish that originated in Kansas City. These bite-sized pieces of tender pork belly are coated in a sweet and sticky sauce, making them a crowd favorite.

Directions

1: In a small bowl, mix together the salt, pepper, garlic powder, onion powder, paprika, and brown sugar.
2: Rub the seasoning mixture all over the pork belly, making sure to cover all sides.
3: Let the pork belly sit at room temperature for 30 minutes.
4: Preheat your smoker to 225°F and add wood chips for flavor.
5: Place the pork belly on the smoker and cook for 4-5 hours, until the internal temperature reaches 190°F.
6: Cut the pork belly into bite-sized pieces and place them in a foil pan.
7: Pour BBQ sauce over the pork belly pieces and toss to coat.
8: Return the pan to the smoker and cook for an additional 1-2 hours.
9: Let the pork belly burnt ends rest for 10 minutes before serving.

French Dip Sandwiches

4 servings · 450 calories · 15 minutes

Ingredients:

- 2 lbs beef chuck roast
- 1 onion, thinly sliced
- 4 cloves garlic, minced
- 1 cup beef broth
- 1/4 cup soy sauce
- 1 tablespoon Worcestershire sauce
- 1 teaspoon dried thyme
- Salt and pepper to taste
- 4 baguettes, sliced
- Provolone cheese slices for topping (optional)

Substitutions

- Add sautéed mushrooms to the sandwich for an extra layer of flavor.
- Use Swiss cheese instead of provolone for a traditional twist.
- Toast the baguette slices for added crunch.

Experience the allure of French cuisine with Slow Cooker French Dip Sandwiches. Succulent roast beef, slow-cooked to perfection, meets crusty baguettes and a savory au jus for a sandwich that is both hearty and satisfying. Let the slow cooker do the work as you savor the classic flavors of a French bistro in the comfort of your home.

Directions

1. Place beef roast, sliced onion, and garlic in the slow cooker.
2. In a bowl, mix beef broth, soy sauce, Worcestershire sauce, thyme, salt, and pepper. Pour over the beef.
3. Cook on low for 6-8 hours until beef is tender.
4. Shred the beef and assemble sandwiches with baguette slices.
5. Optionally, top with provolone cheese and broil until melted.
6. Dip the sandwiches into the savory au jus and relish the French-inspired feast.

Buffalo Chicken Wraps

4 servings   **320** calories   **20** minutes

Ingredients:

- 1 1/2 lbs boneless, skinless chicken breasts
- 1 cup Buffalo sauce
- 1/2 cup ranch dressing
- 1 cup shredded lettuce
- 1 cup diced tomatoes
- 1/2 cup crumbled blue cheese
- 4 large flour tortillas
- 1/4 cup chopped green onions
- Salt and pepper to taste

Substitutions

- Adjust Buffalo sauce quantity to your spice preference.
- Use blue cheese dressing for added creaminess.
- Wrap in lettuce leaves for a low-carb option.

Spice up your mealtime routine with Buffalo Chicken Wraps. Inspired by the fiery flavors of Buffalo wings, these wraps are a zesty delight. Slow-cooked chicken bathed in tangy Buffalo sauce, wrapped in a tortilla—it's a culinary escapade that brings the excitement of game day to your table.

Directions

1. Place chicken breasts in the slow cooker and pour Buffalo sauce over them. Cook on low for 4 hours.
2. Shred the chicken and mix with ranch dressing.
3. Assemble wraps with shredded lettuce, diced tomatoes, blue cheese, and Buffalo chicken mixture.
4. Sprinkle with green onions and season with salt and pepper.
5. Wrap and enjoy the spicy goodness.

Tip: Serve with celery sticks for a classic pairing.

Sesame Crispy Tofu Salad

1 serving   30 minutes

Savor the Sesame Crispy Tofu Salad—a crunchy delight where golden tofu meets the nuttiness of sesame. A dish that's not just a salad but a vegan symphony of flavors!
A vegan symphony of flavors to tantalize your taste buds!

Ingredients:

- 200g firm tofu, cubed
- 2 tbsp sesame seeds
- 2 cups mixed greens
- 1/2 cup shredded carrots
- 1/4 cup edamame
- 2 tbsp sesame ginger dressing
- 1 tbsp soy sauce
- 1 tbsp rice vinegar
- Salt and pepper to taste

Directions

1. Press tofu to remove excess water, then coat with sesame seeds.
2. In a pan, sauté sesame-coated tofu until golden brown.
3. In a bowl, toss mixed greens, shredded carrots, and edamame.
4. In a small bowl, whisk together sesame ginger dressing, soy sauce, and rice vinegar.
5. Drizzle the dressing over the salad.
6. Top with sesame-crusted tofu.
7. Enjoy the vegan symphony of flavors!

Insider Tips

Add a handful of crispy fried onions for an extra crunch.
Drizzle with sriracha for a spicy kick.

Eggplant Rollatini

4 servings   45 minutes

Immerse yourself in the elegance of Eggplant Rollatini, where thin slices of eggplant are rolled around a savory ricotta filling.

Ingredients:

- 1 large eggplant, thinly sliced lengthwise
- 1 tablespoon olive oil
- 1 cup ricotta cheese
- 1/2 cup grated Parmesan cheese
- 1 egg, beaten
- 1 teaspoon dried oregano
- 1 teaspoon dried basil
- 2 cups marinara sauce
- 1 cup mozzarella cheese, shredded
- Fresh basil for garnish

Substitutions

- Choose small to medium-sized eggplants for more manageable slices.
- Add ground meat to the marinara sauce for a heartier dish.
- Make it ahead of time and bake just before serving for a stress-free meal.
- Serve with a side of sautéed spinach or a light salad.

Directions

1. Preheat oven to 375°F (190°C).
2. Brush eggplant slices with olive oil and bake for 15-20 minutes until tender.
3. In a bowl, combine ricotta cheese, Parmesan cheese, beaten egg, dried oregano, and dried basil.
4. Spread a spoonful of marinara sauce on each eggplant slice.
5. Place a dollop of the ricotta mixture at one end and roll the eggplant slice.
6. Arrange the rolls in a baking dish.
7. Pour the remaining marinara sauce over the rolls.
8. Top with shredded mozzarella cheese.
9. Bake for 20-25 minutes or until bubbly.
10. Garnish with fresh basil.
11. Enjoy the sophistication of Eggplant Rollatini.

Sausage and Cabbage Stir-Fry

4 servings   **25 minutes**

This Sausage and Cabbage Stir-Fry is a quick and satisfying low-carb dish. Savory sausage meets crisp cabbage in a flavorful stir-fry that's perfect for busy evenings.

Ingredients:

- 1 lb smoked sausage, sliced
- 1 small head cabbage, shredded
- 1 onion, sliced
- 1 bell pepper, sliced
- 2 cloves garlic, minced
- 2 tbsp soy sauce
- 1 tsp ginger, grated
- 2 tbsp olive oil

Directions

1. Heat olive oil in a large skillet.
2. Add sausage and cook until browned.
3. Add onion, bell pepper, and garlic. Sauté until vegetables are tender.
4. Stir in cabbage.
5. Mix soy sauce and ginger, pour over the mixture.
6. Cook until cabbage is wilted.
7. Serve and enjoy the simplicity of a flavorful stir-fry.

Insider Tips

Cooking Hack: Opt for low-sodium soy sauce if you're watching your salt intake.

Bell Pepper Nachos

4 servings   **20** minutes

Experience the joy of Bell Pepper Nachos, where vibrant bell peppers serve as the perfect vessel for your favorite toppings.

Ingredients:

- 4 large bell peppers, halved and seeded
- 1 lb ground turkey
- 1 packet taco seasoning
- 1 cup shredded cheddar cheese
- 1/2 cup diced tomatoes
- 1/4 cup sliced green onions
- 1/4 cup sliced olives
- Sour cream and guacamole for topping

Directions

1. Preheat the oven to 375°F (190°C).
2. Brown ground turkey in a pan and season with taco seasoning.
3. Place bell pepper halves on a baking sheet.
4. Spoon the seasoned turkey into each bell pepper half.
5. Top with shredded cheddar cheese.
6. Bake for 15 minutes or until cheese is melted and bubbly.
7. Remove from the oven and sprinkle with diced tomatoes, sliced green onions, and sliced olives.
8. Serve with dollops of sour cream and guacamole.
9. Enjoy the vibrant Bell Pepper Nachos.

Insider Tips

Cooking Hack: Customize with your favorite nacho toppings. The bell pepper boats bring a colorful crunch; let them be the vibrant maestros.

Loaded Cauliflower Bake

1 serving   **25 minutes**

Ingredients:

- 2 cups cauliflower florets
- 1/2 cup shredded cheddar cheese
- 3 slices cooked bacon, crumbled
- 2 green onions, chopped

Unveil the magic of cauliflower with this Loaded Cauliflower Bake. A low-carb delight with the richness of cheese, bacon, and green onions.

Directions

1. Steam cauliflower until tender.
2. Mix in cheese, bacon, and green onions.
3. Bake until cheese melts and bubbles.
4. Serve hot.

Insider Tips

Cooking Hack: Pre-cook cauliflower for a quicker bake. Experiment with different cheese blends for a flavor twist.

Nutella Stuffed Crepes

2 crepes   30 minutes

Ingredients:

1 cup all-purpose flour
2 eggs
1 1/4 cups milk
2 tbsp melted butter
Pinch of salt
Nutella for filling
Powdered sugar for dusting

Thin crepes filled with rich Nutella spread, a decadent treat for breakfast or dessert.

Directions

1. In a blender, combine flour, eggs, milk, melted butter, and salt. Blend until smooth.
2. Heat a non-stick skillet over medium heat and lightly grease with butter.
3. Pour a small amount of batter onto the skillet and swirl to coat the bottom evenly.
4. Cook until the edges start to lift and the bottom is golden brown.
5. Flip the crepe and cook the other side briefly.
6. Remove crepe from the skillet and spread Nutella on one half.
7. Fold the crepe in half, then in quarters.
8. Repeat with the remaining batter and Nutella.
9. Dust crepes with powdered sugar before serving.

Insider Tips

Cooking Hacks: You can add sliced bananas or strawberries along with Nutella for extra flavor. Adjust the sweetness by adding more or less Nutella to each crepe.

S'mores Breakfast Burrito

1 burrito   25 minutes

Ingredients:

1 large flour tortilla
2 eggs (scrambled)
2 tbsp chocolate chips
2 tbsp mini marshmallows
1 tbsp graham cracker crumbs
1 tbsp butter

A unique twist on the classic s'mores, wrapped in a warm tortilla for a delightful breakfast experience.

Directions

1. In a skillet, melt butter over medium heat.
2. Add scrambled eggs and cook until set.
3. Sprinkle chocolate chips, mini marshmallows, and graham cracker crumbs over the eggs.
4. Cook until marshmallows start to melt.
5. Warm the tortilla in a separate skillet or microwave.
6. Place the egg mixture in the center of the tortilla.
7. Roll the tortilla to form a burrito.
8. Serve warm and enjoy the s'mores goodness!

Insider Tips

Cooking Hacks: You can use a tortilla wrap that's slightly toasted for a crispier texture. Adjust the amount of chocolate chips and marshmallows to suit your taste preferences.

www.ingramcontent.com/pod-product-compliance
Ingram Content Group UK Ltd
Pitfield, Milton Keynes, MK11 3LW, UK
UKRC030822271025
8603UKWH00039B/398

9 798349 552281